TRACEABLE LETTERS AND NUMBERS FOR PRESCHOOL.

HANDWRITING PRACTICE BOOK FOR KIDS

TRACE THE ALPHABET

Trace the cell completely, to reveal the letter A

TRACE THE NUMBER

Trace the cell completely, to reveal the number 1

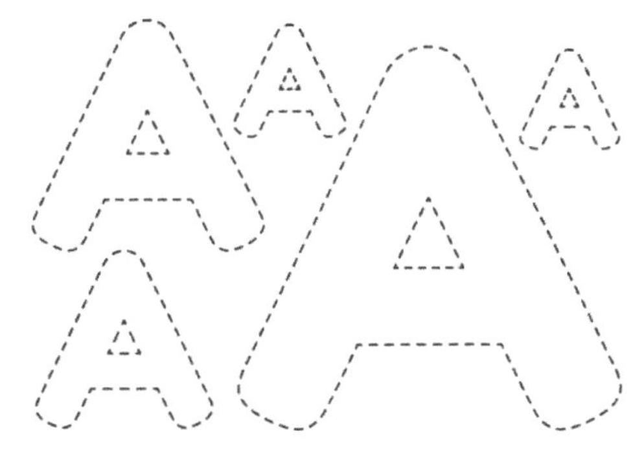

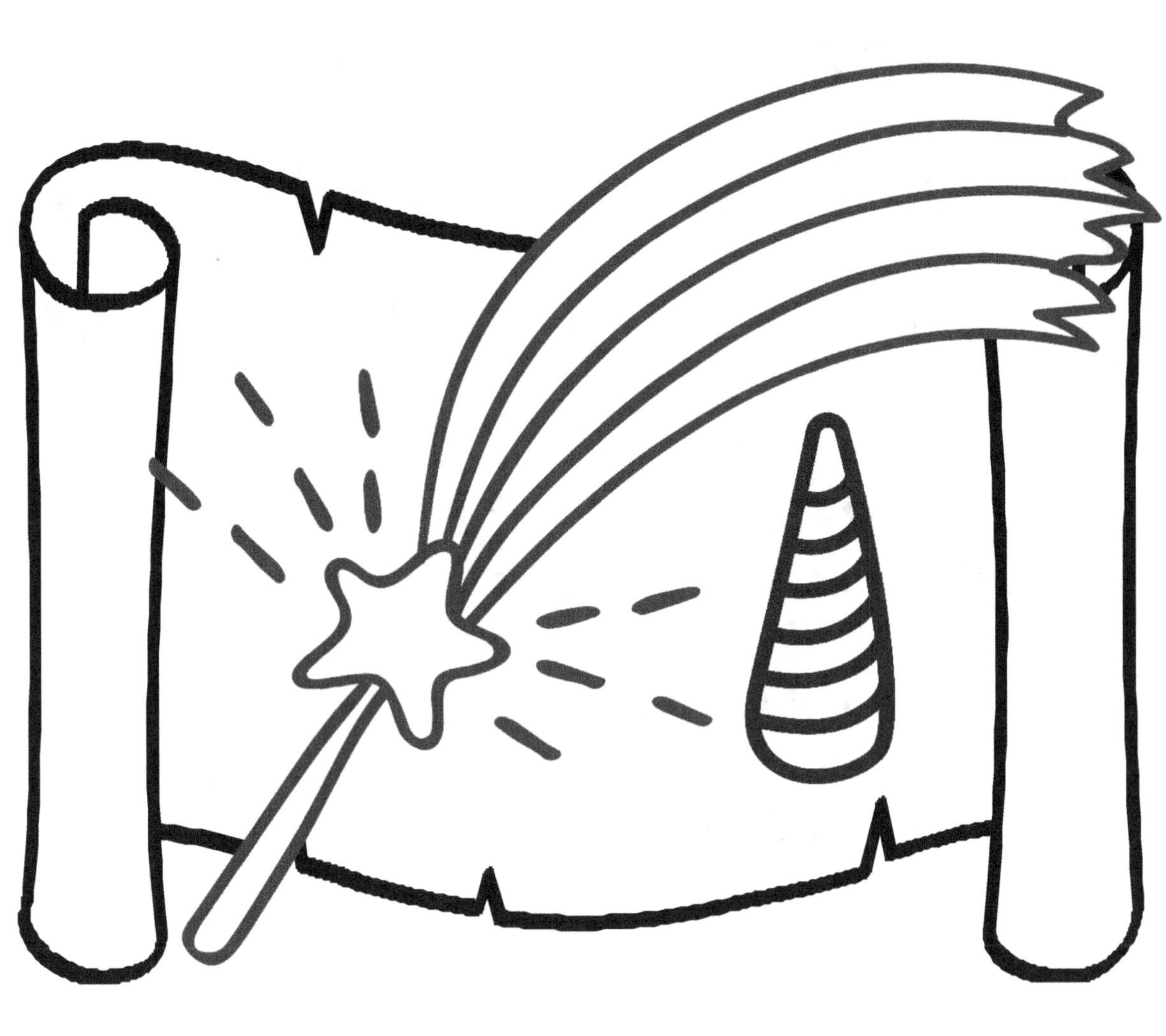

This Activity Book Belongs To:

____

____

____

DESCRIPTION

Prek/Kindergarten handwriting book, focusing on numbers and letter practice. Give children one letter and one number a day tracing and activity

Worksheets. Skills: Writing letters A-Z (upper and lower case), The worksheets include:

Alphabet activity worksheets:
- Learn the Alphabets A-Z lower case and upper case letters
- Letter-sound practice
- Find and color each alphabet.

Number activity worksheets:
- Number tracing, writing numbers 1-10, number recognition,
- Find and color each number.

The worksheets can be put in a binder and made into a morning workbook for preschool students' daily work. One letter and one number a day!

Test Your Colors Here

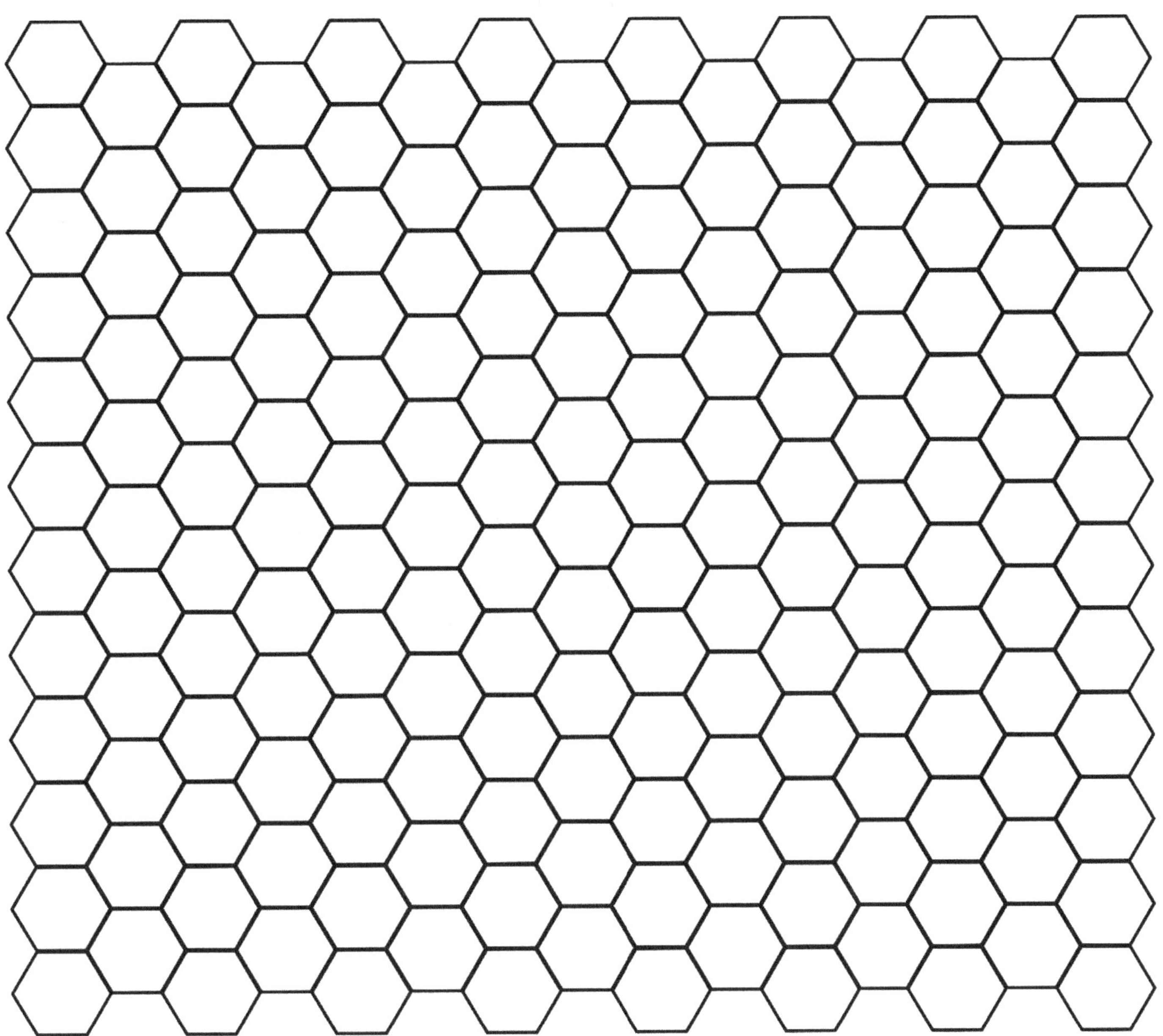

Are you using markers? To minimize bleed-through,
consider adding a blank sheet of paper
behind each coloring page.

TRACE THE ALPHABET

Trace the cell completely, to reveal the letter A

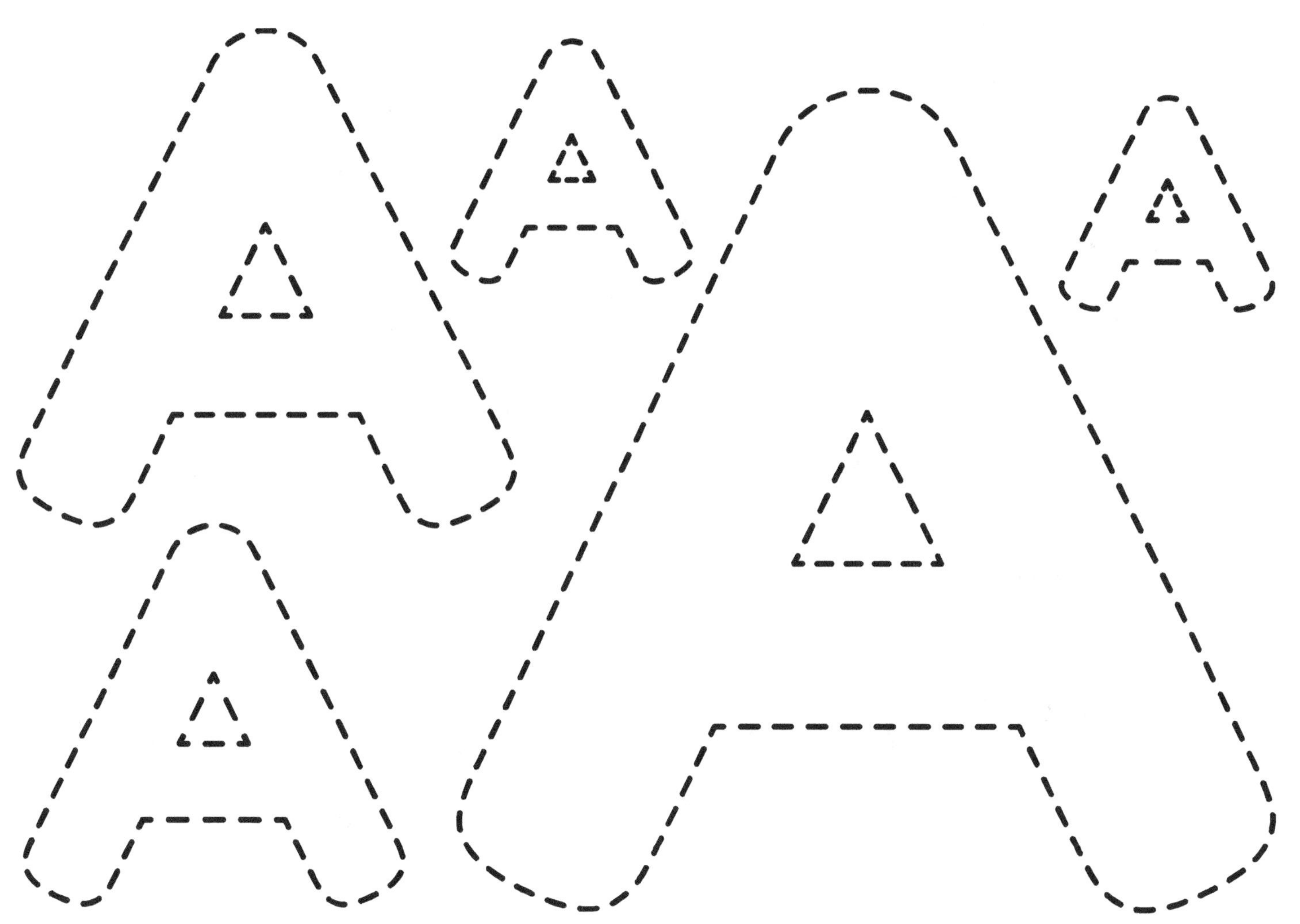

Read, Trace, Write and read the words again

Name: _______________

Date: _______________

Trace:

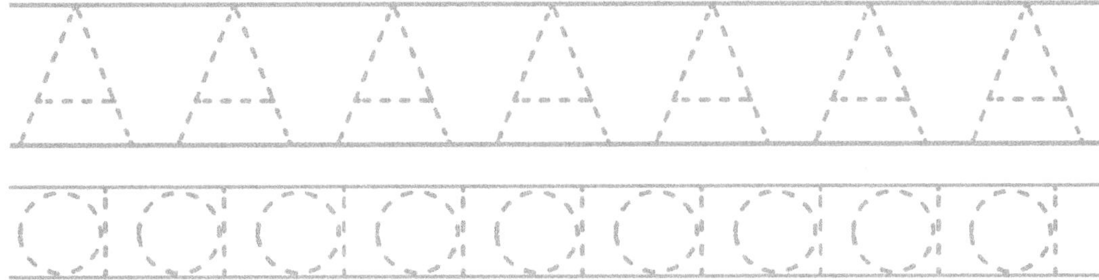

Find and color A:

TRACE THE ALPHABET

Trace the cell completely, to reveal the letter B

Read, Trace, Write and read the words again

Name:

Date:

Trace:

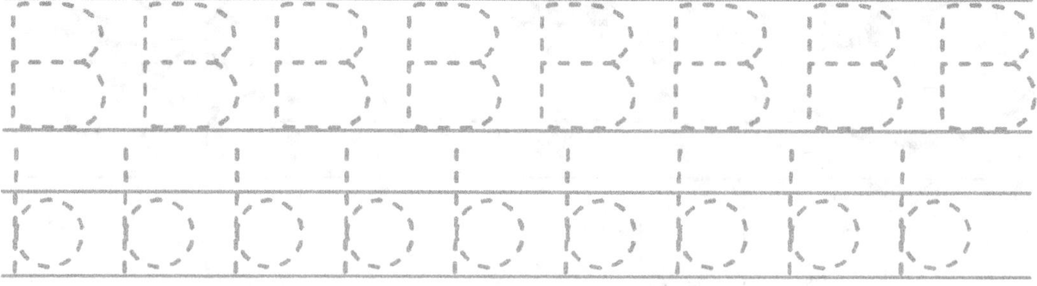

Find and color B:

TRACE THE ALPHABET

Trace the cell completely, to reveal the letter C

Read, Trace, Write and read the words again

Trace:

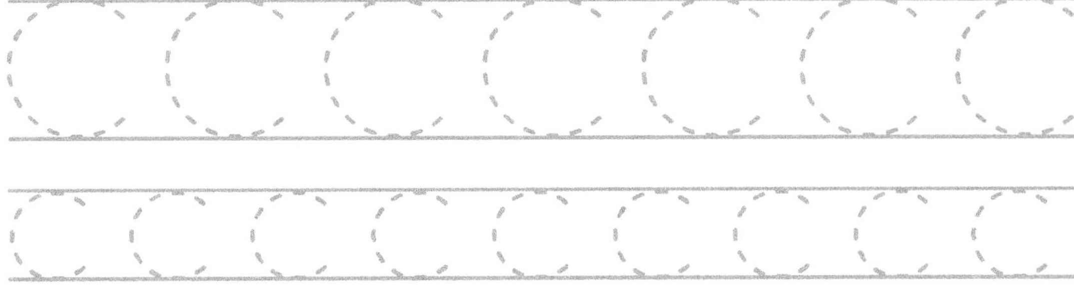

Find and color C:

TRACE THE ALPHABET

Trace the cell completely, to reveal the letter D

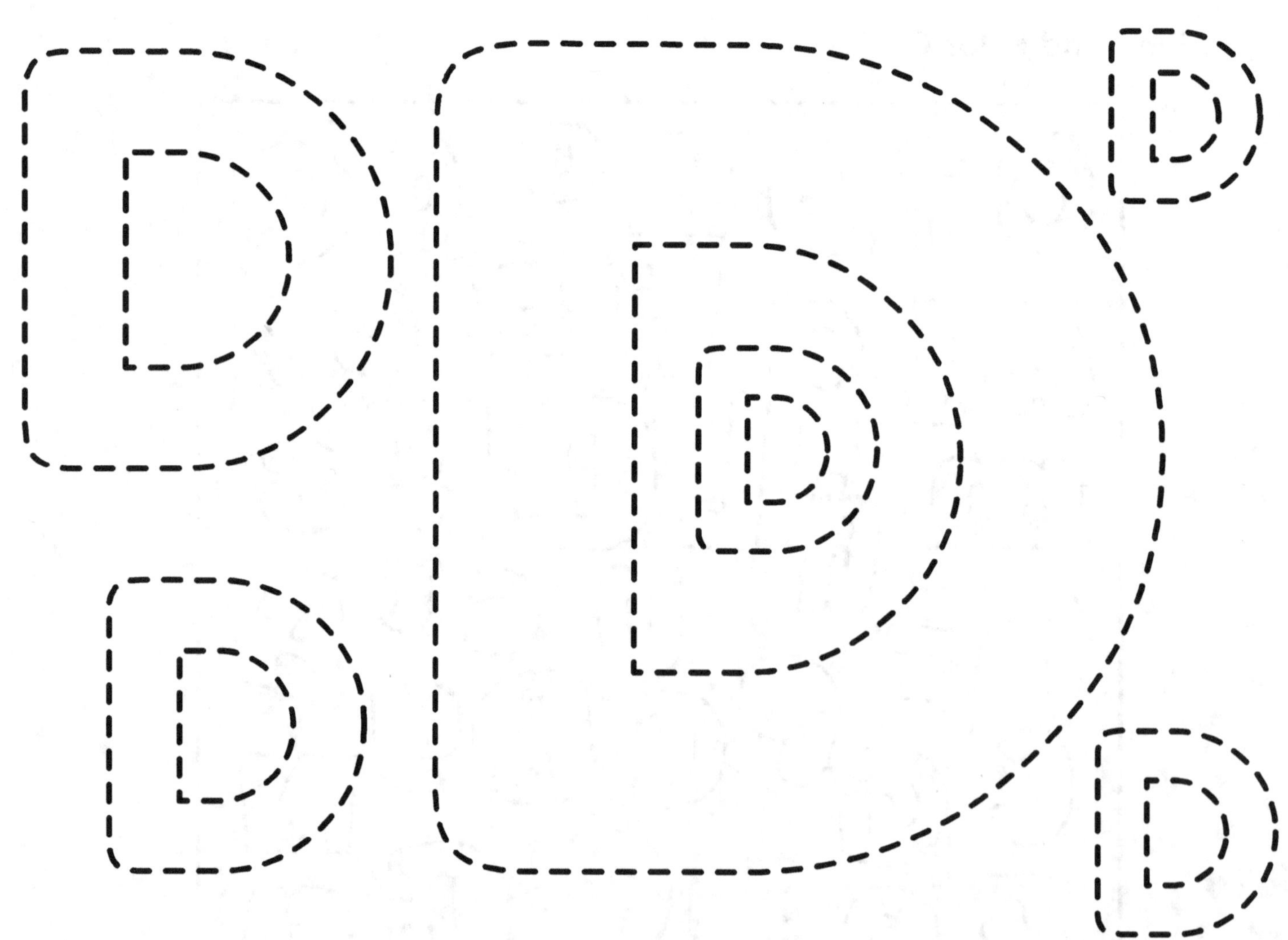

Read, Trace, Write and read the words again

Door

Dinosaur

Dragon Fruit

Name:

Date:

Trace:

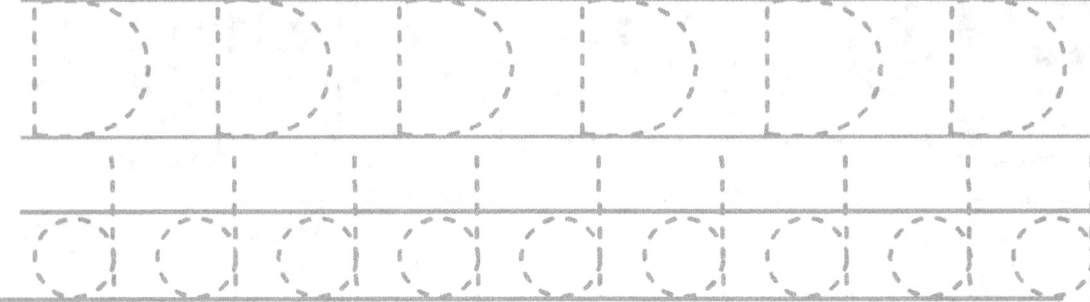

Find and color D:

TRACE THE ALPHABET

Trace the cell completely, to reveal the letter E

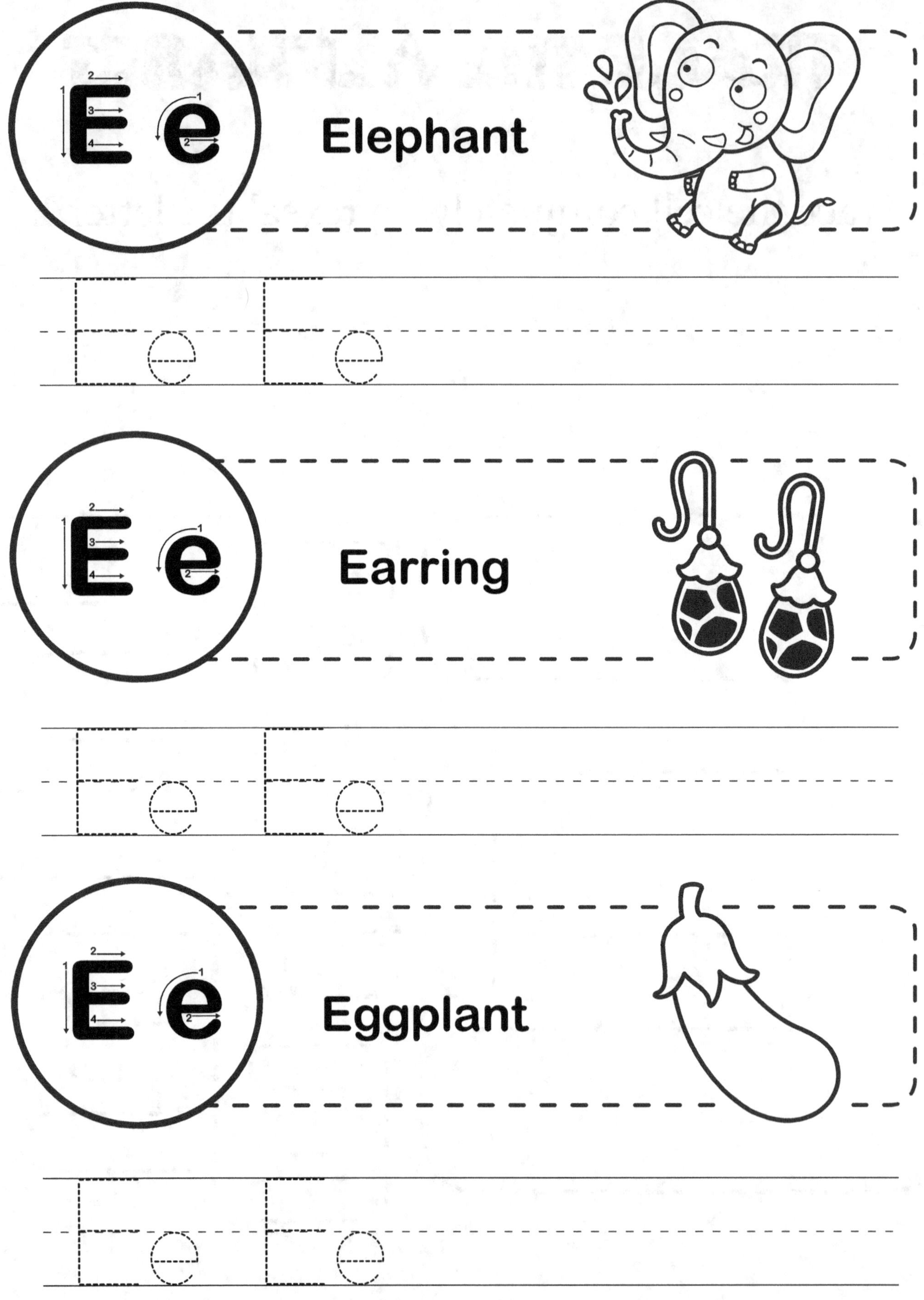

Elephant

Earring

Eggplant

Trace:

Find and color E:

TRACE THE ALPHABET

Trace the cell completely, to reveal the letter F

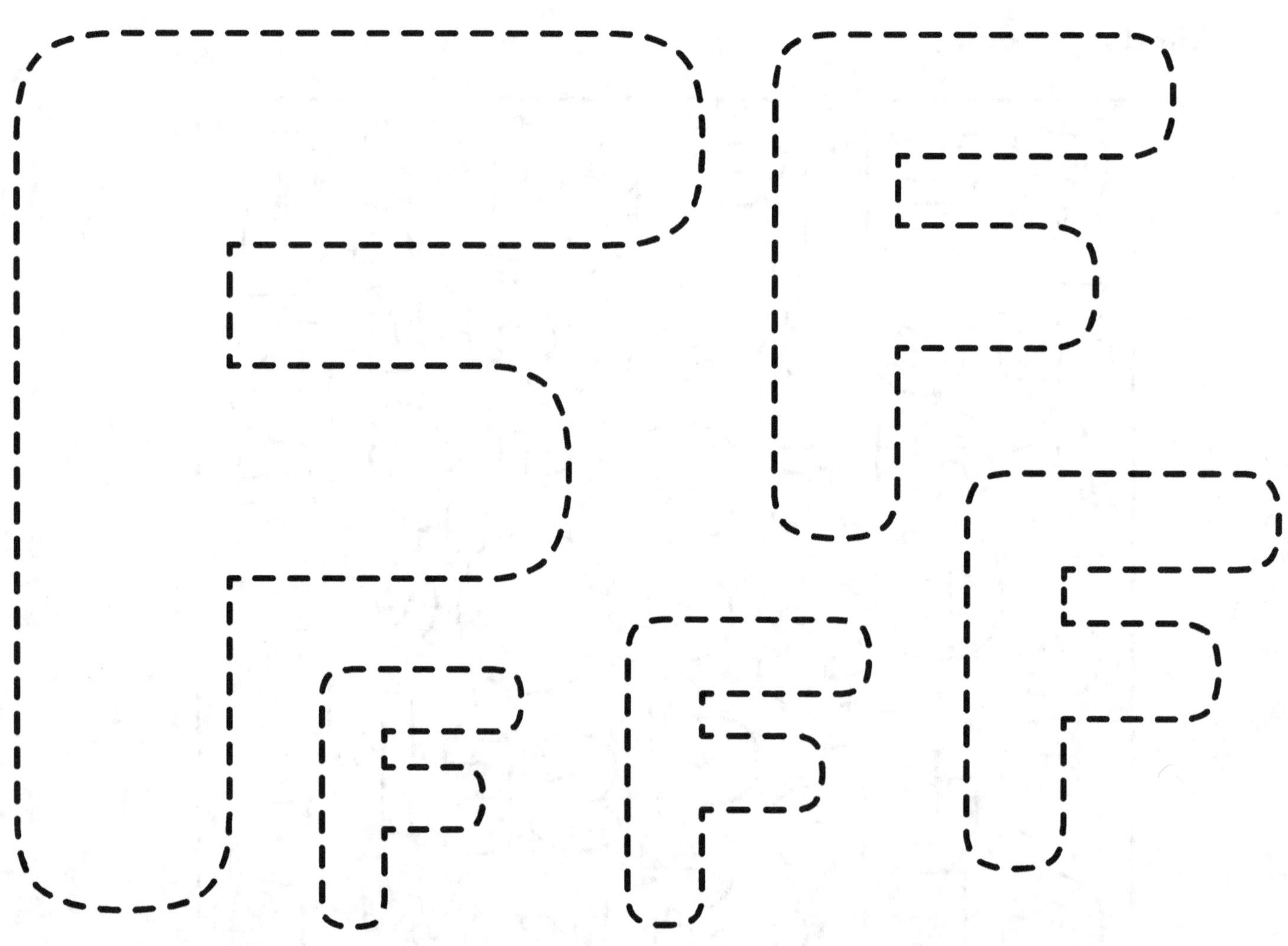

Fence

Fox

Fig

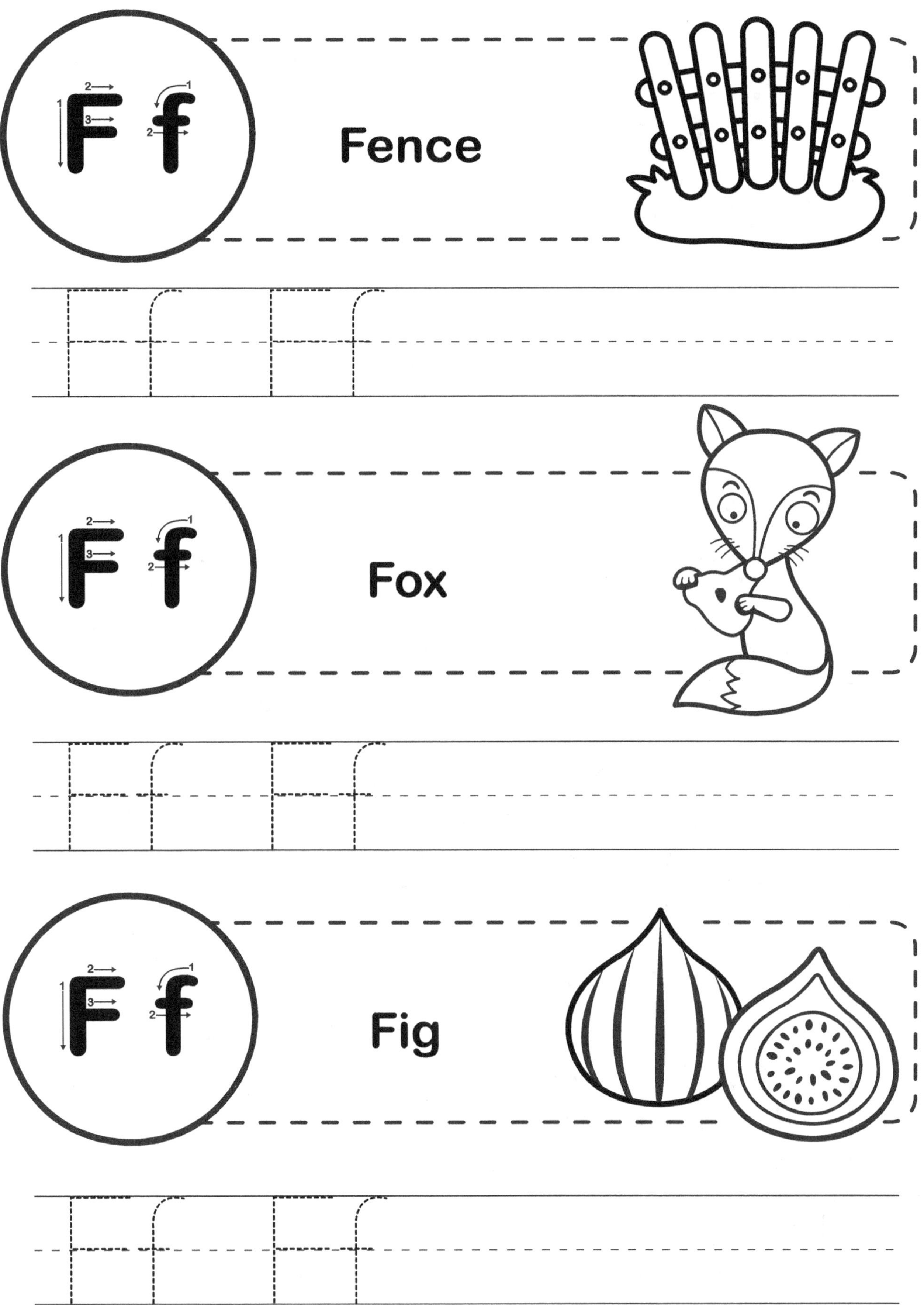

Name:

Date:

Trace:

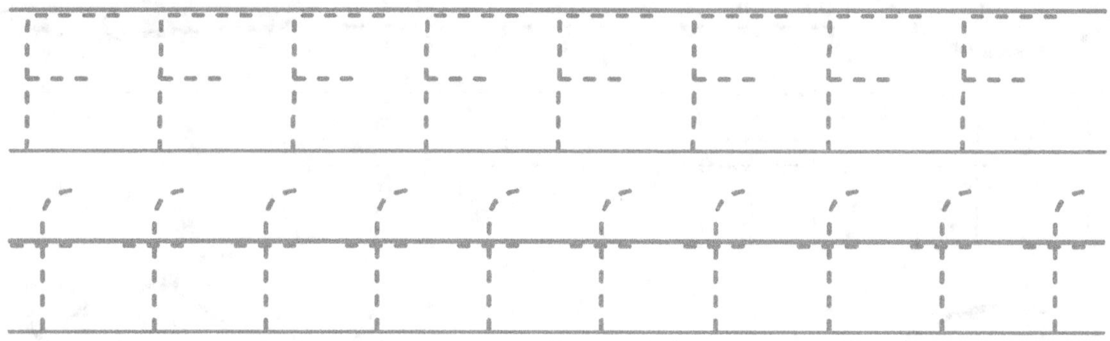

Find and color F:

TRACE THE ALPHABET

Trace the cell completely, to reveal the letter G

Gg
Giraffe
Gg
Garbag Can
Gg
Grapes

Trace:

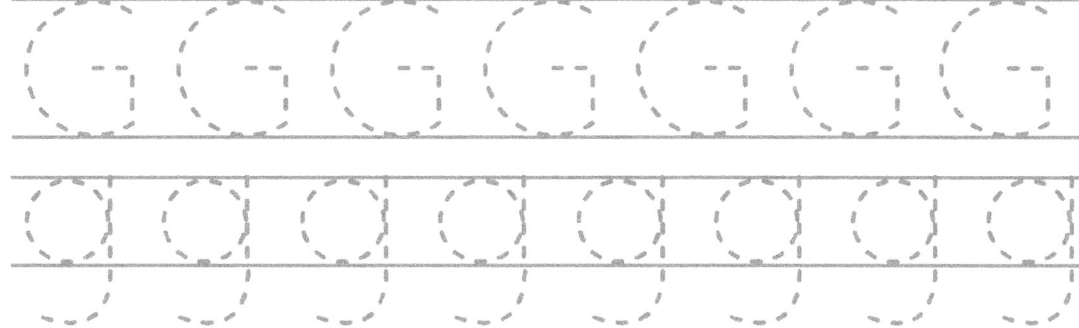

Find and color G:

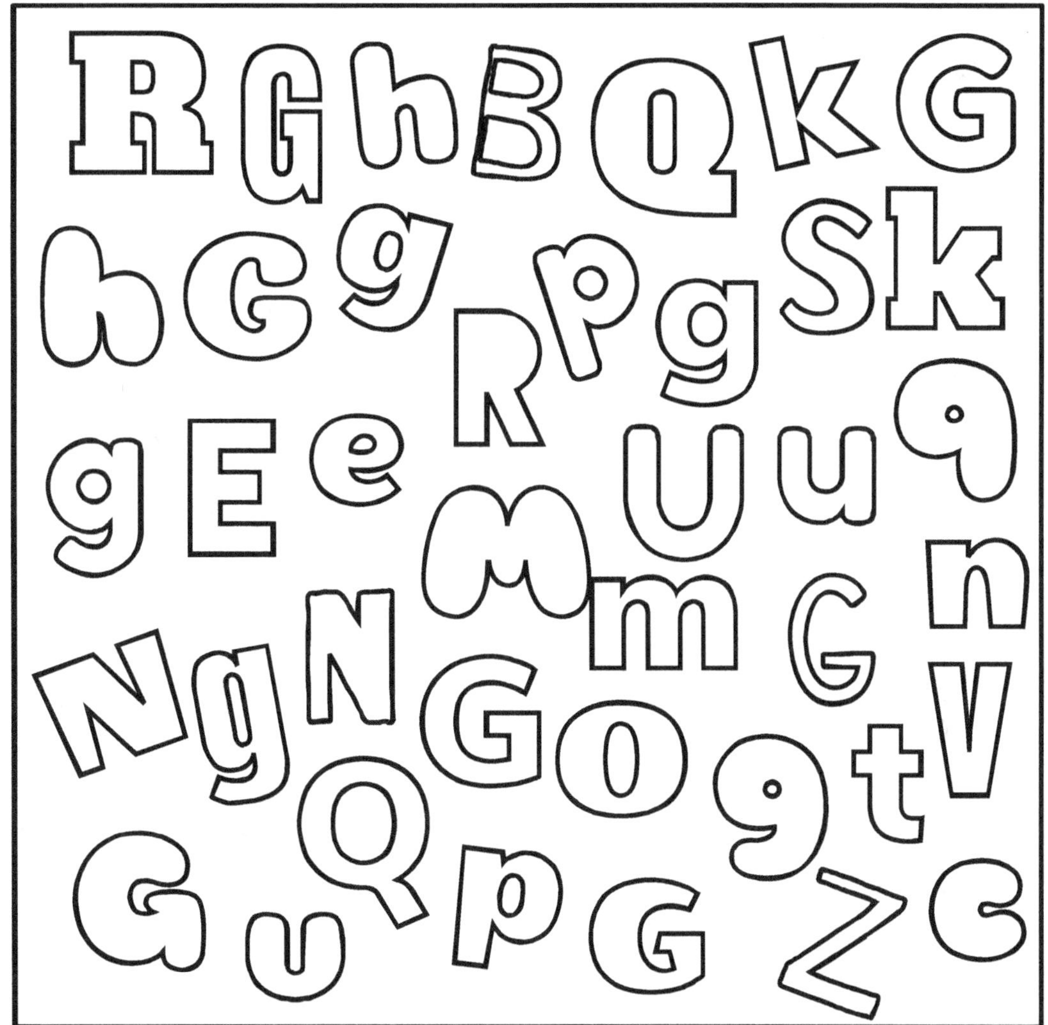

TRACE THE ALPHABET

Trace the cell completely, to reveal the letter H

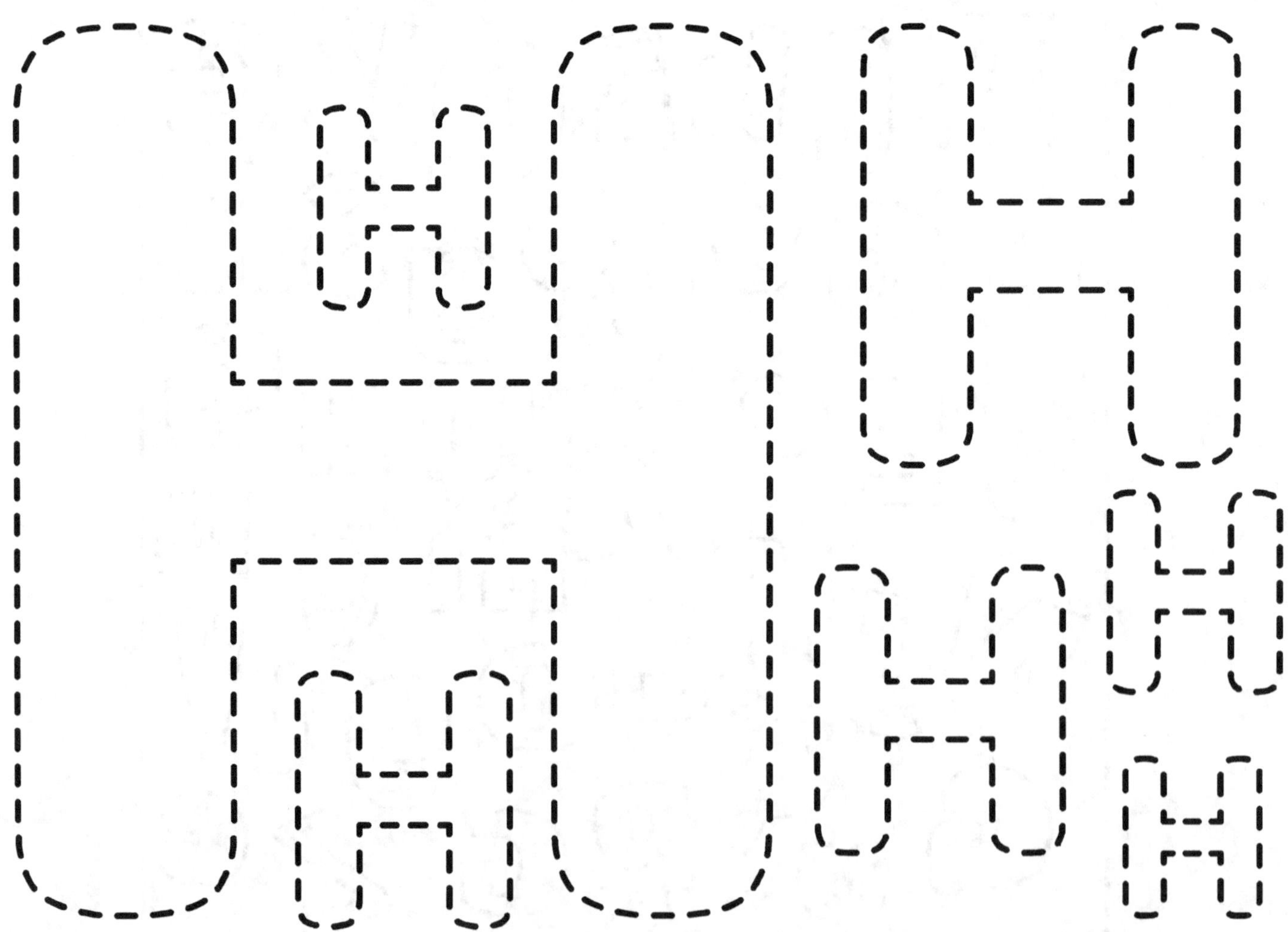

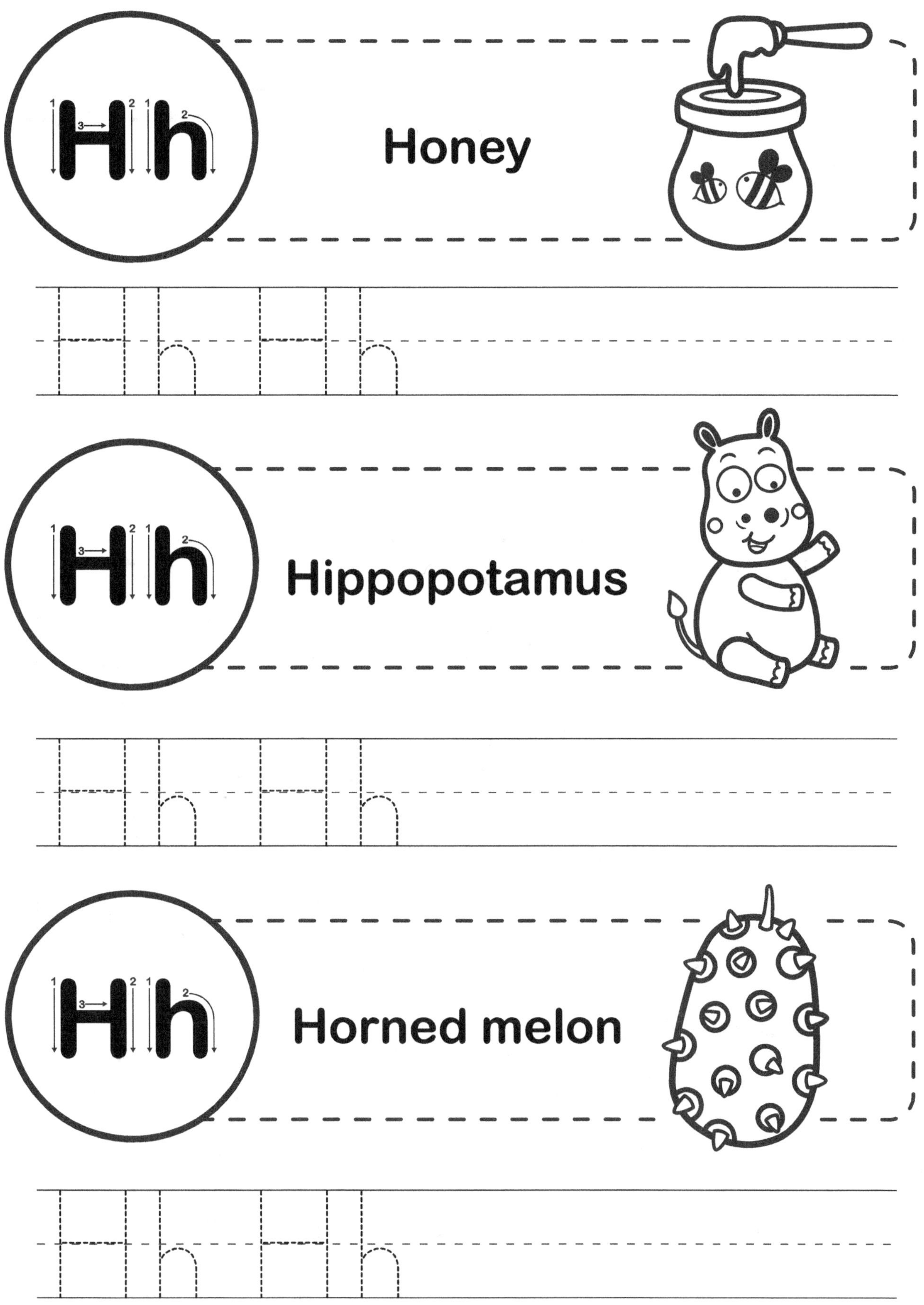
Honey
Hippopotamus
Horned melon

Name: ___________

Date: ___________

Trace:

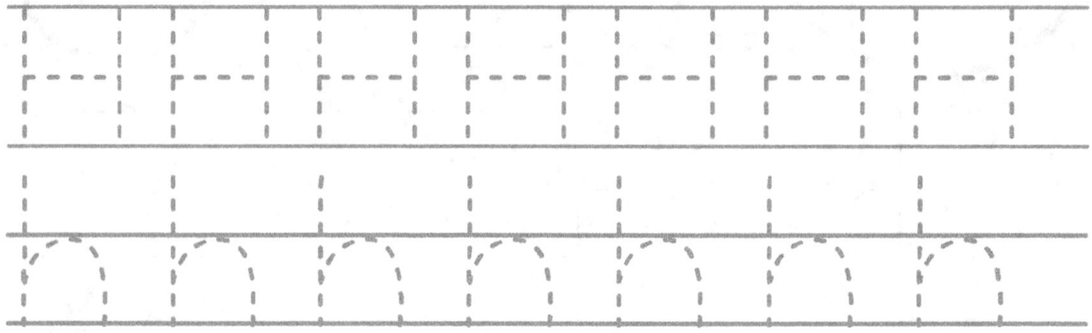

Find and color H:

TRACE THE ALPHABET

Trace the cell completely, to reveal the letter I

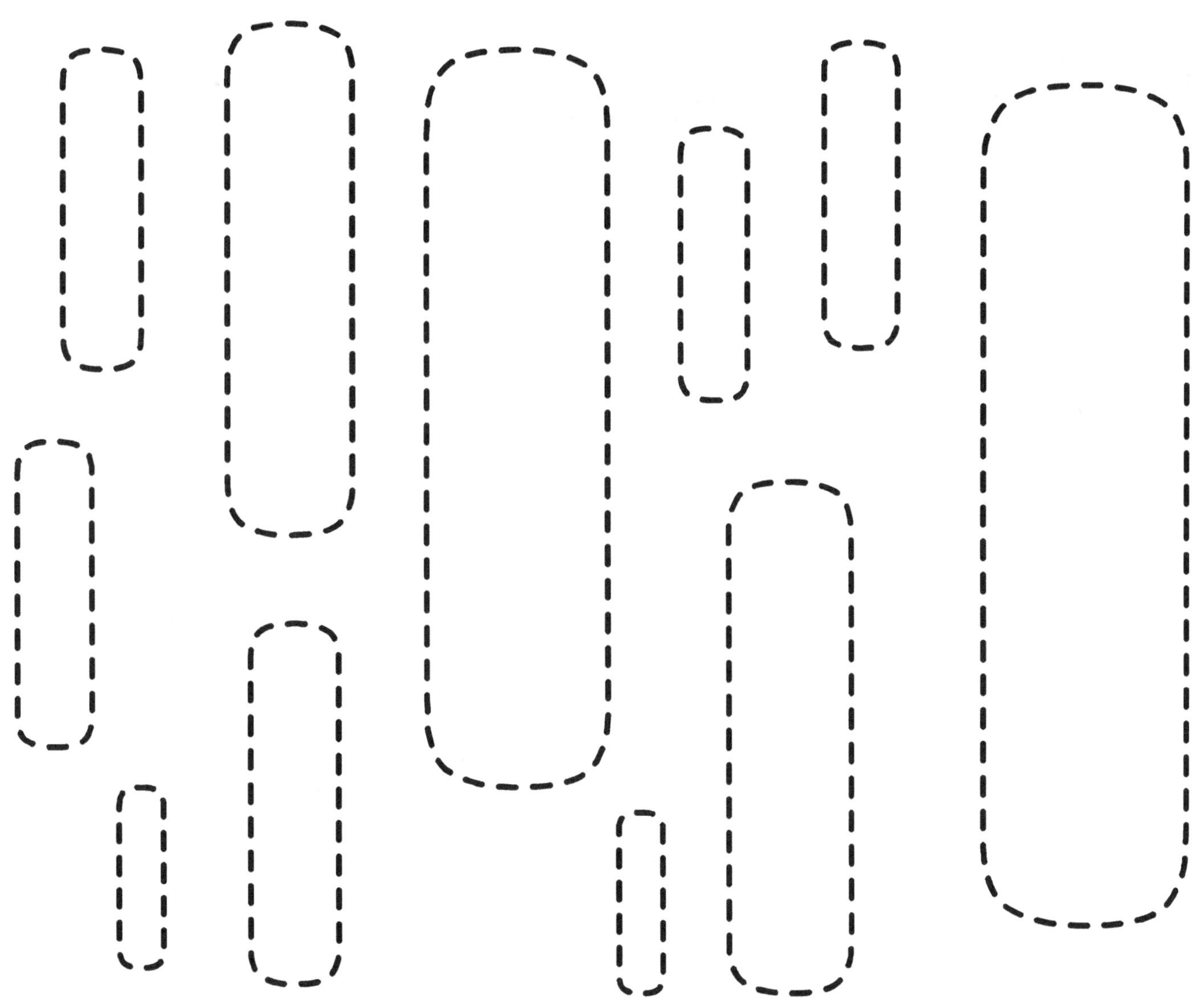

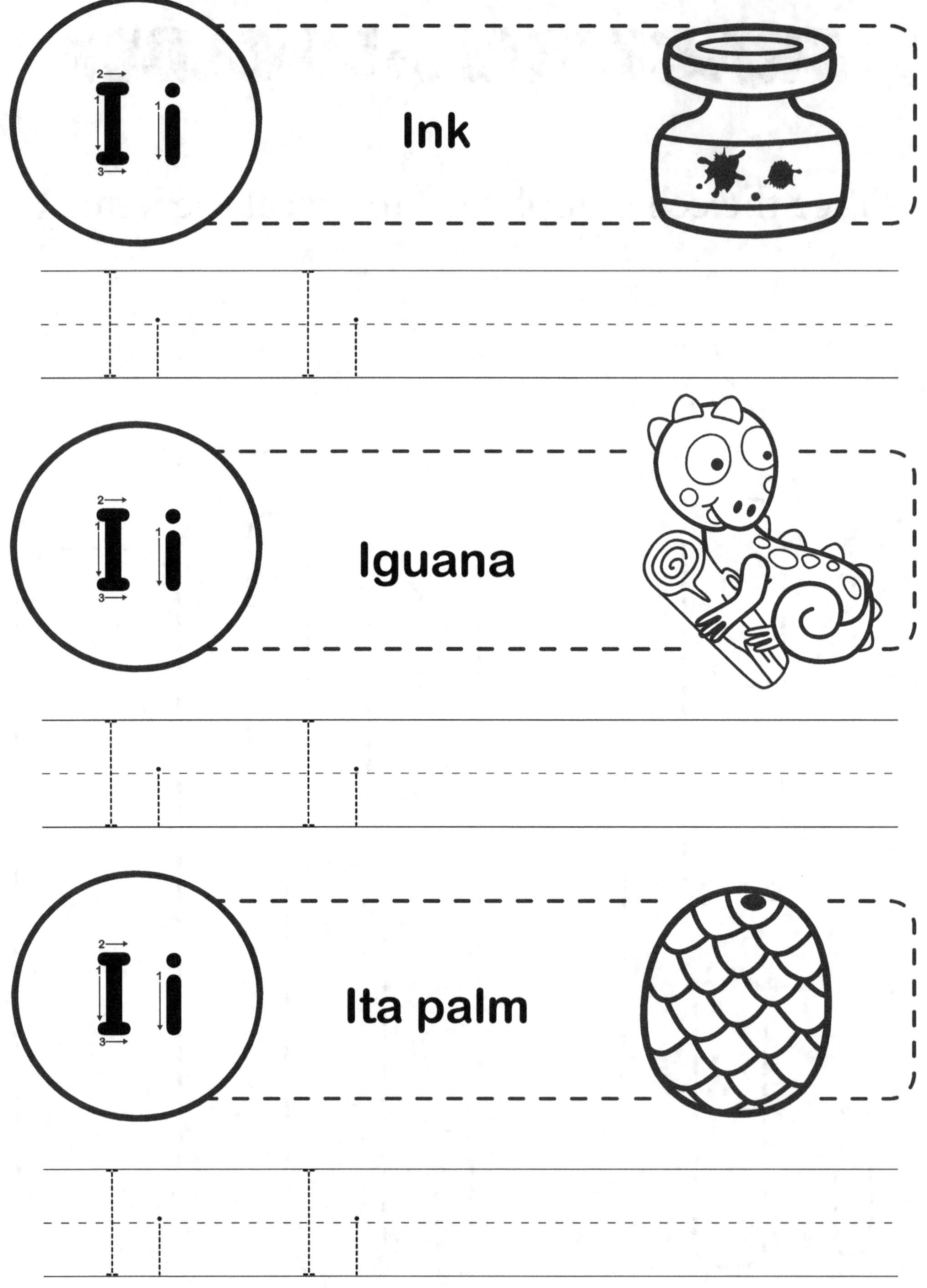
Ink
Iguana
Ita palm

Trace:

Find and color I:

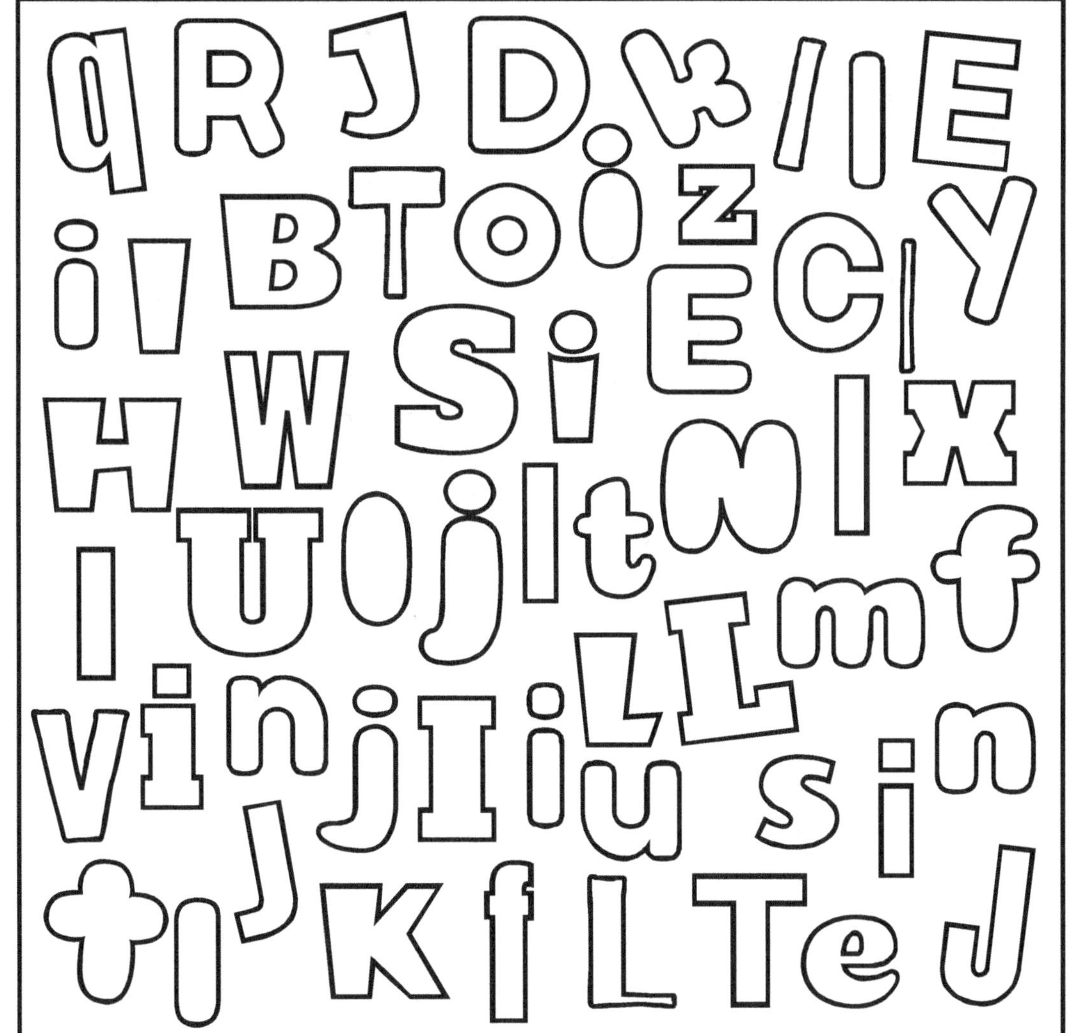

TRACE THE ALPHABET

Trace the cell completely, to reveal the letter J

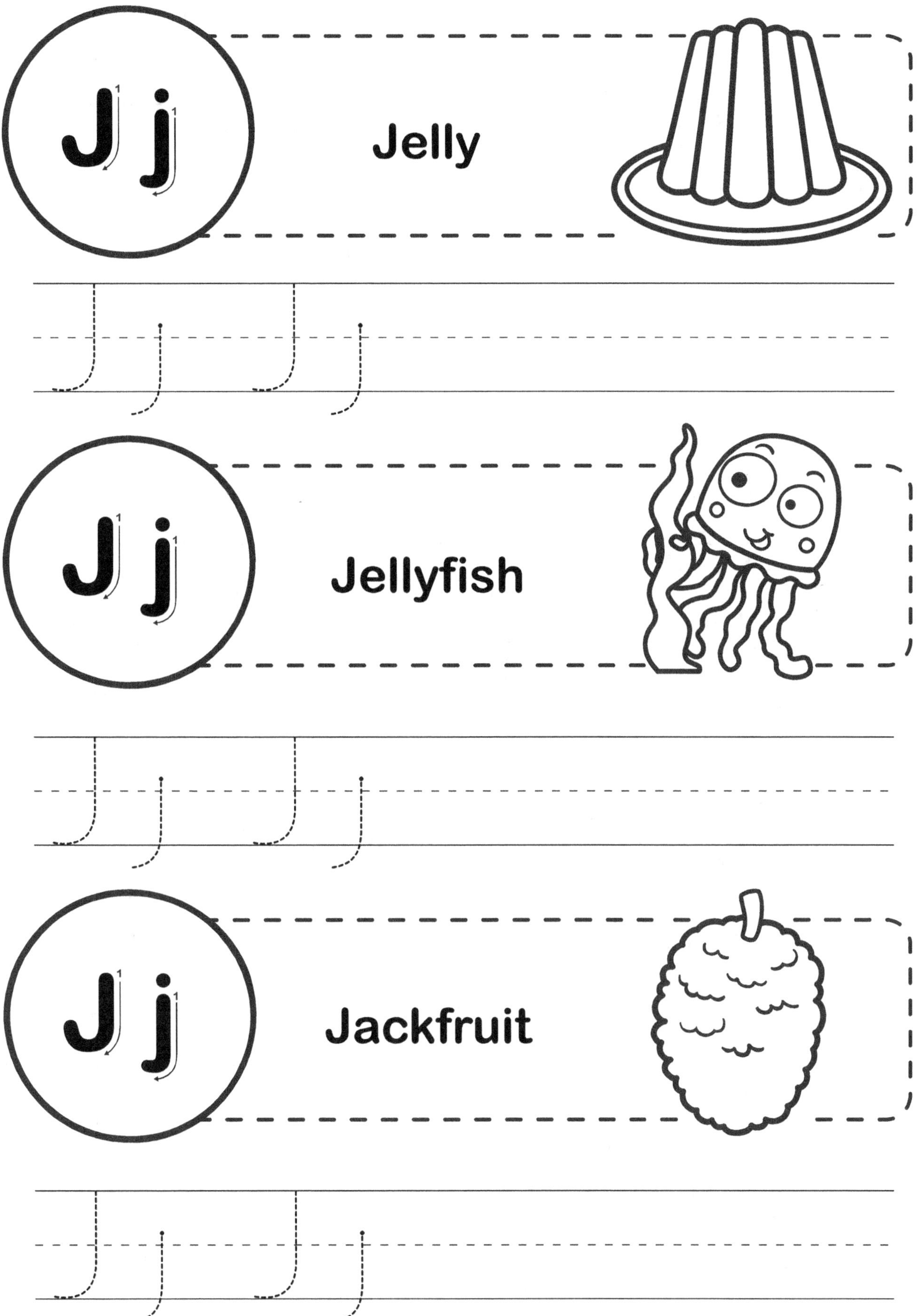

J j Jelly

J j Jellyfish

J j Jackfruit

Trace:

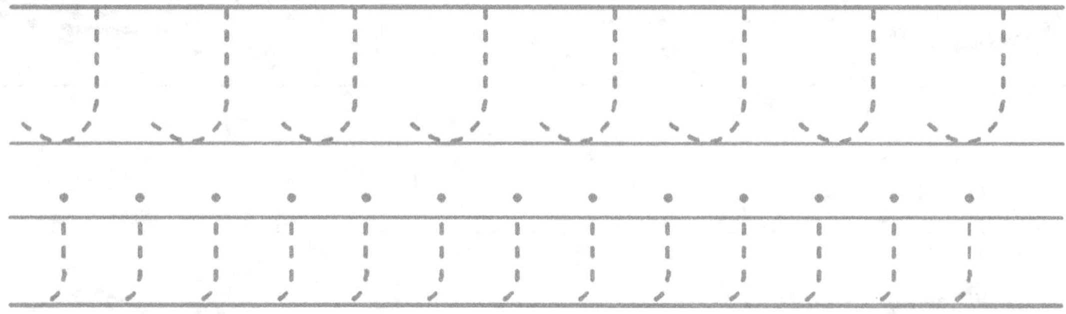

Find and color J:

TRACE THE ALPHABET

Trace the cell completely, to reveal the letter K

K k
Kettle
K k
Kangaroo
K k
Kiwi

Name: _______________

Date: _______________

Trace:

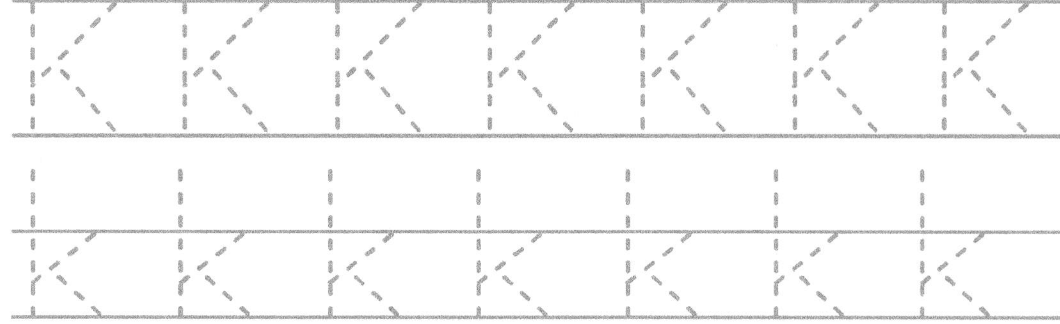

Find and color K:

TRACE THE ALPHABET

Trace the cell completely, to reveal the letter L

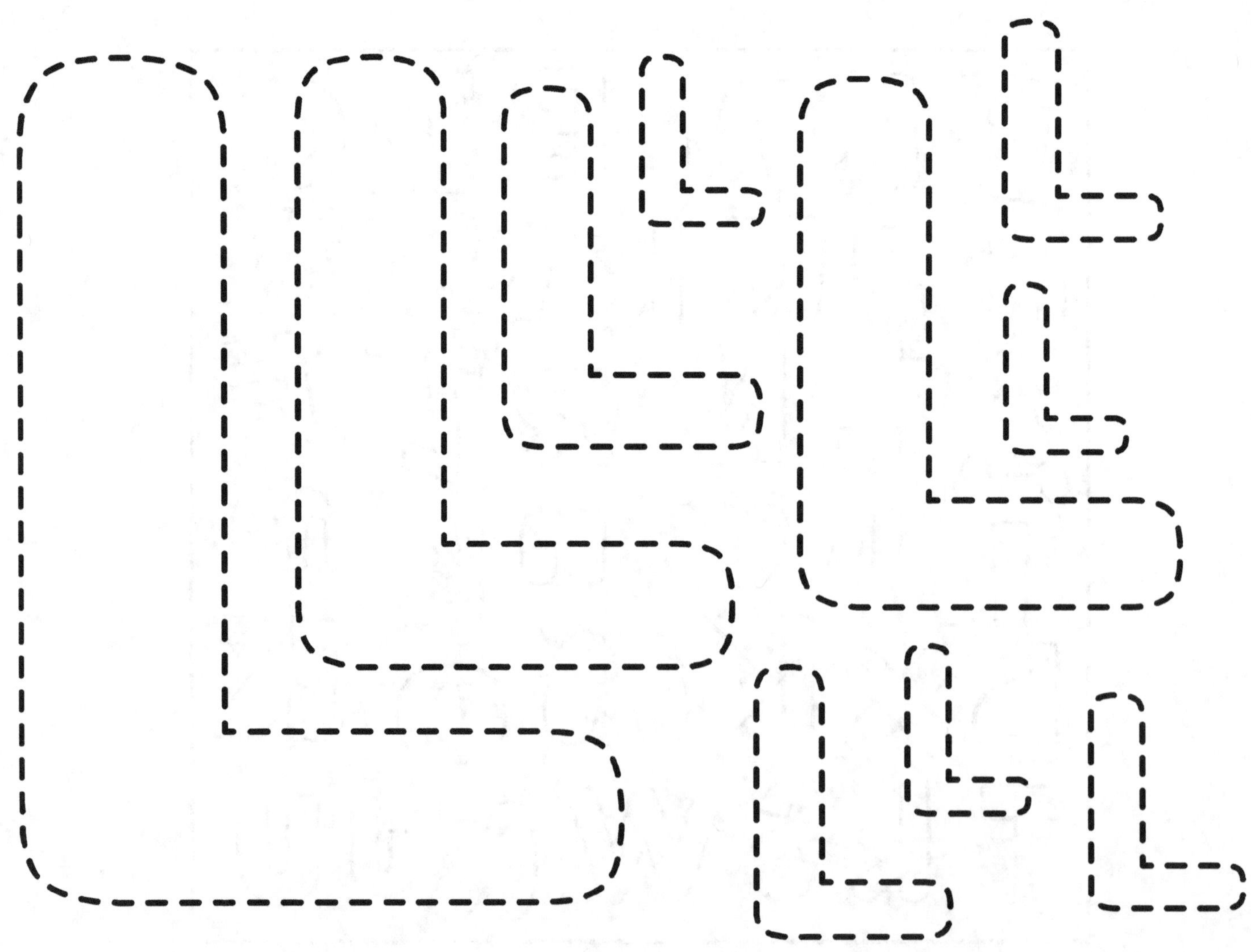

Log

Lion

Lemon

Trace:

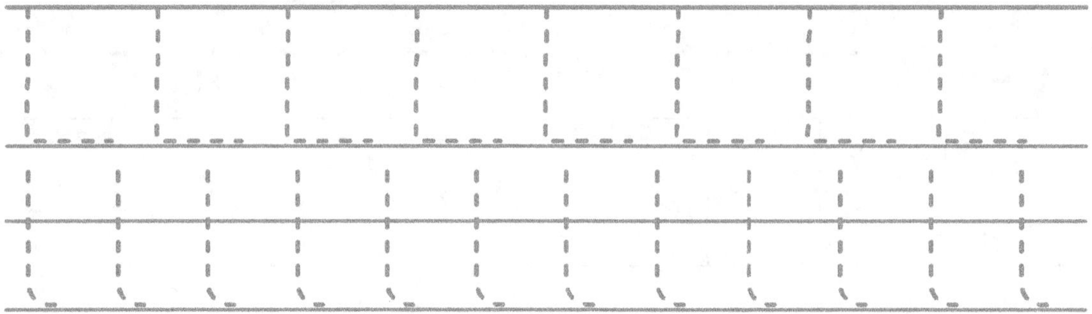

Find and color L:

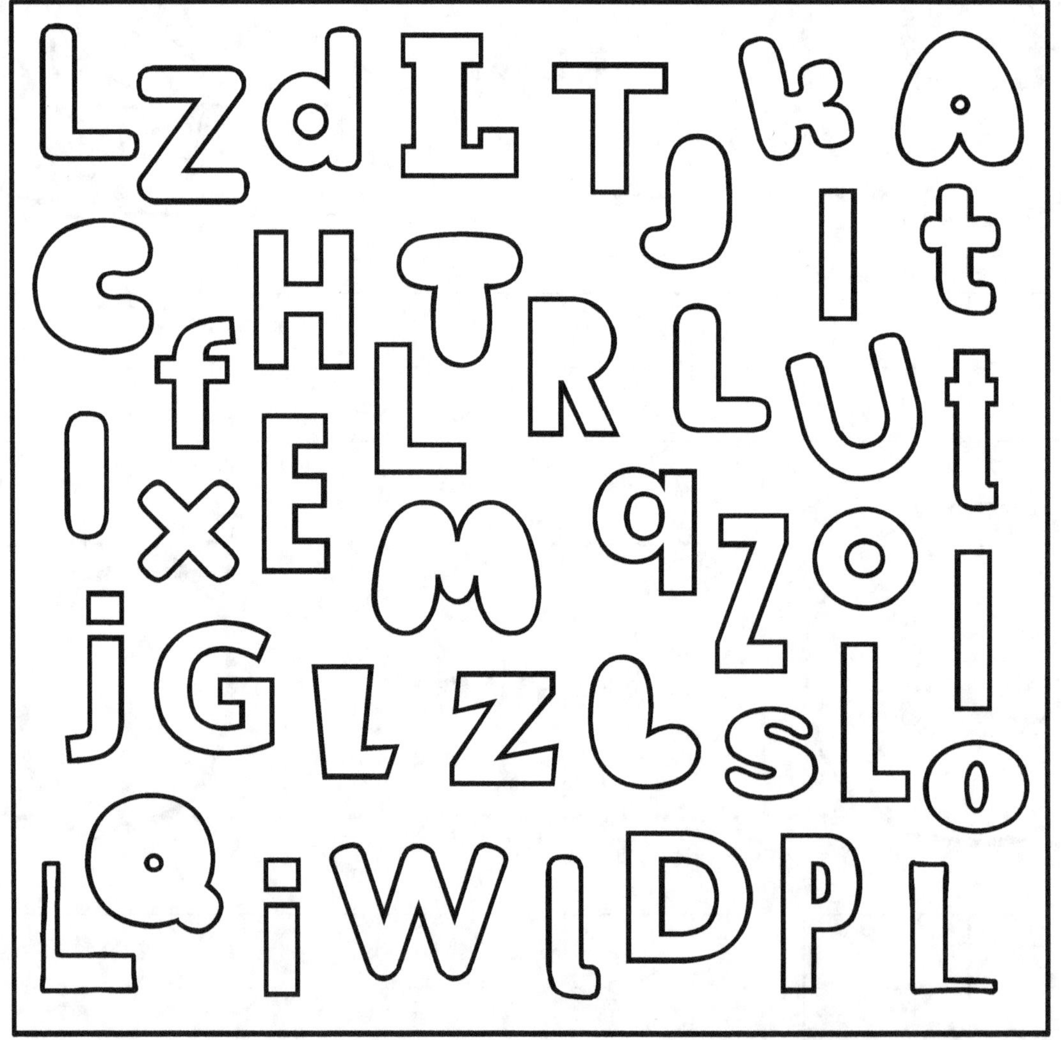

TRACE THE ALPHABET

Trace the cell completely, to reveal the letter M

M m

Mask

M m

Monkey

M m

Mango

Name:

Date:

Trace:

M M M M M M M

m m m m m m m

Find and color M:

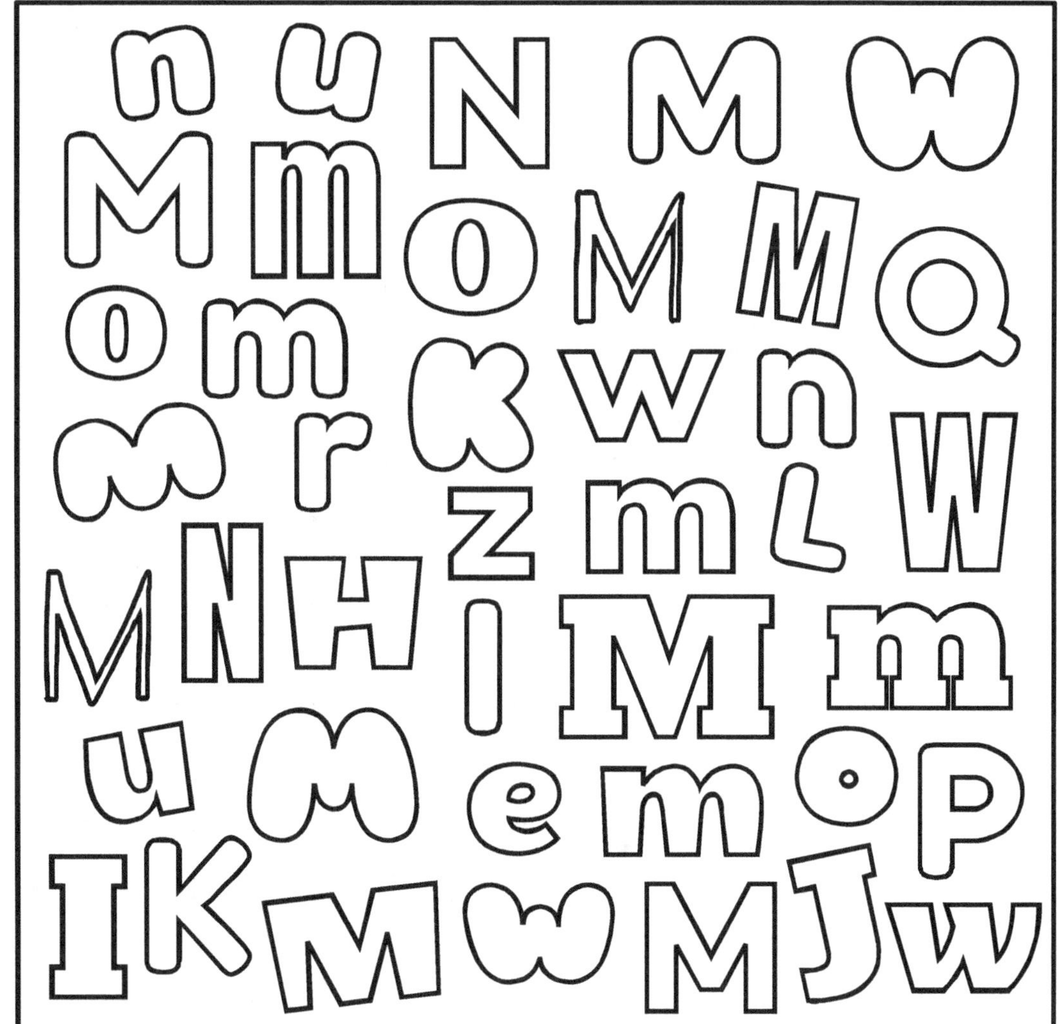

TRACE THE ALPHABET

Trace the cell completely, to reveal the letter N

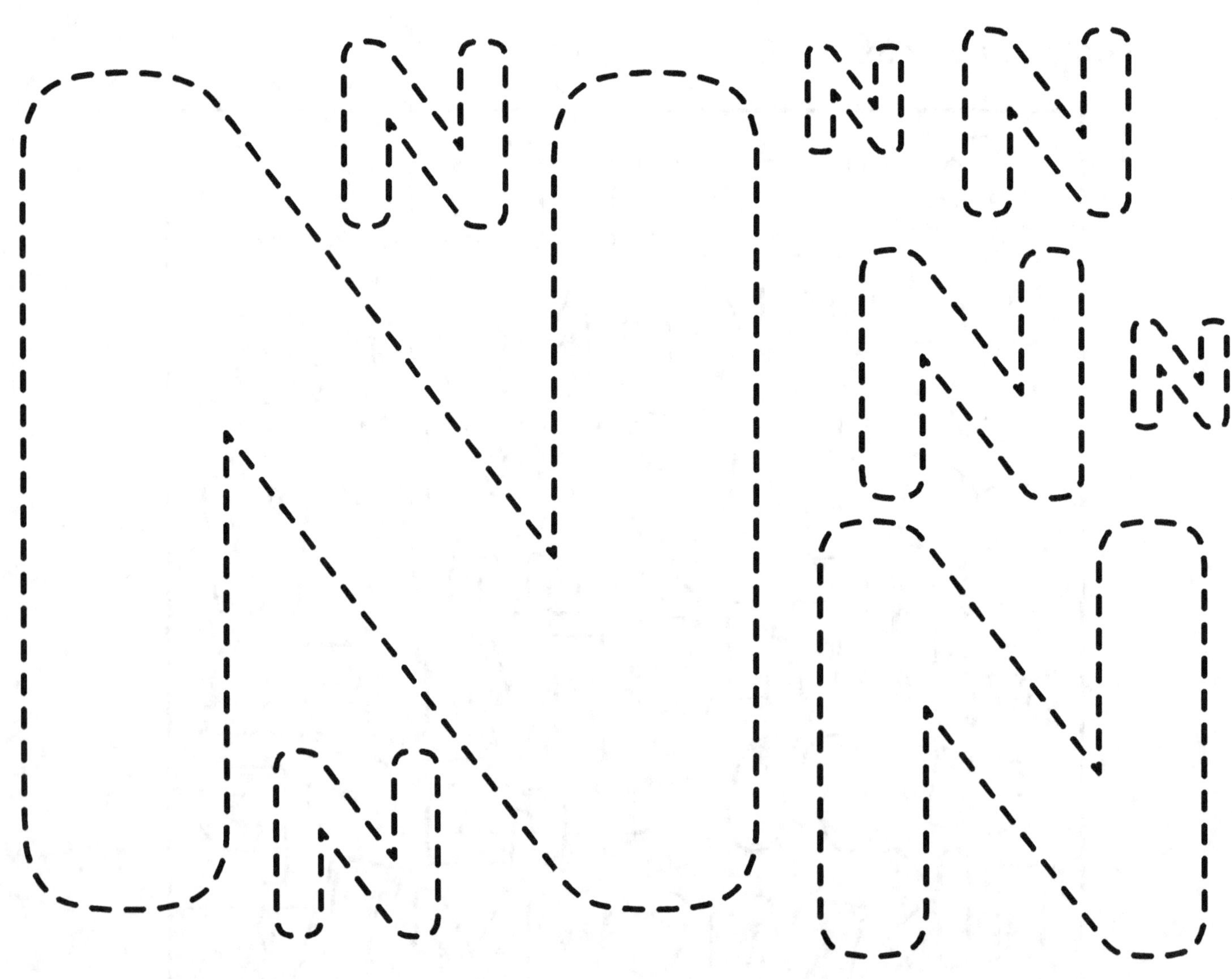

Necklace
Newt
Nungu

N

Trace:

Find and color N:

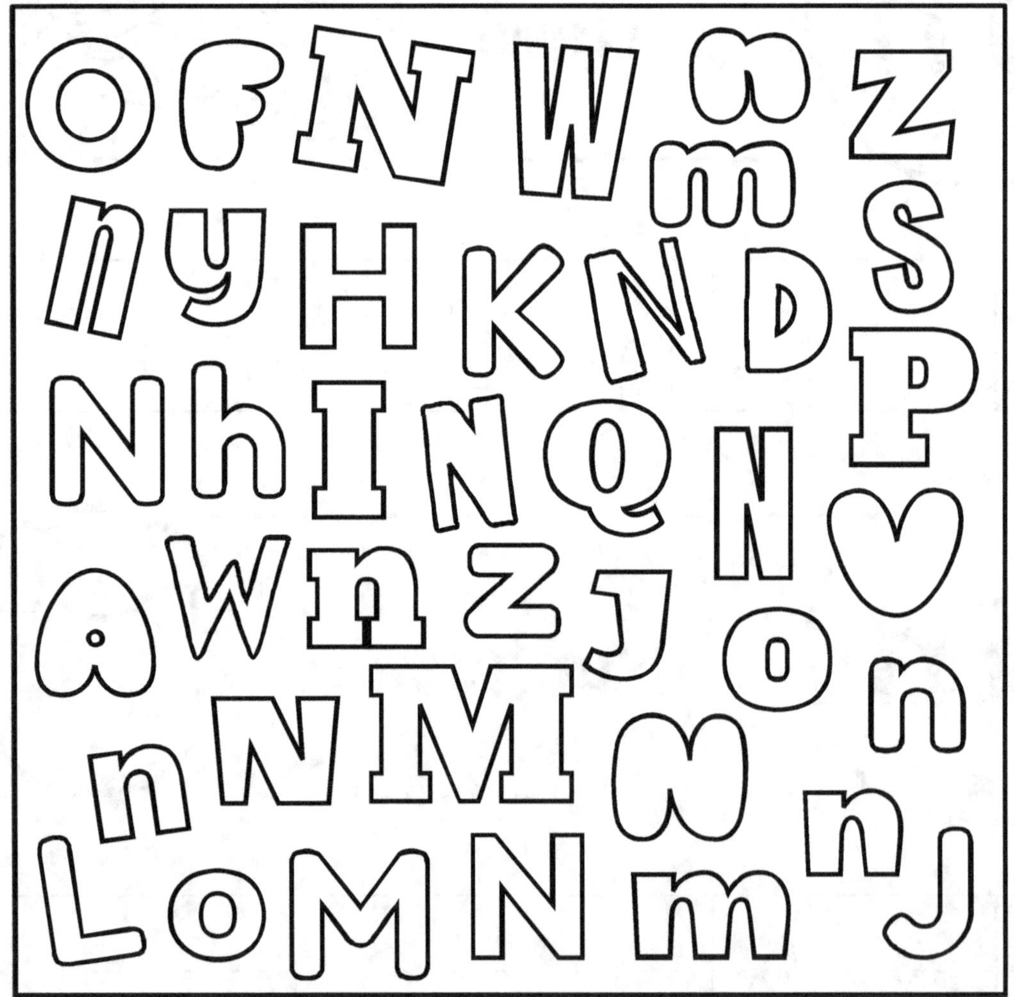

TRACE THE ALPHABET

Trace the cell completely, to reveal the letter O

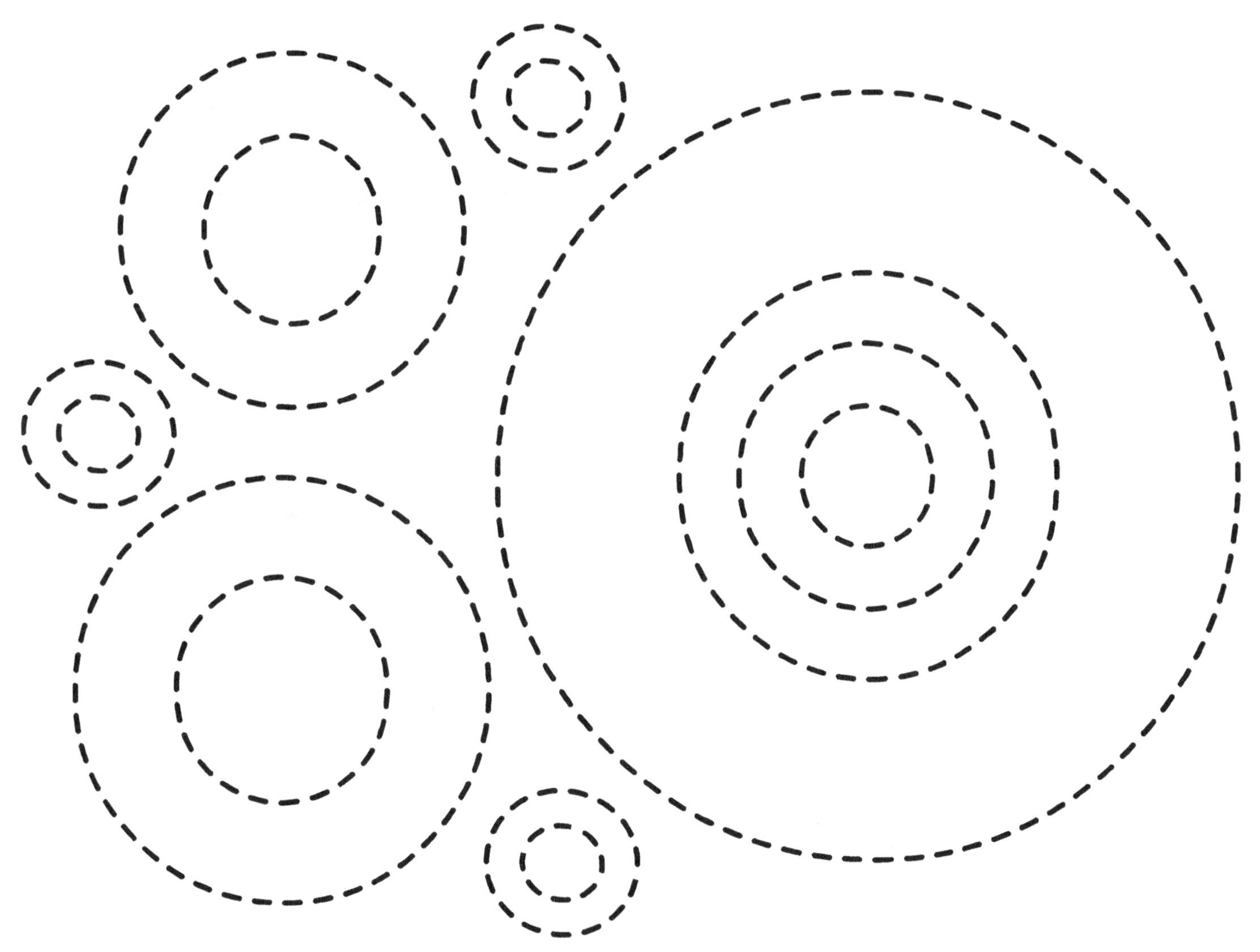

Oil
Owl
Orange

Trace:

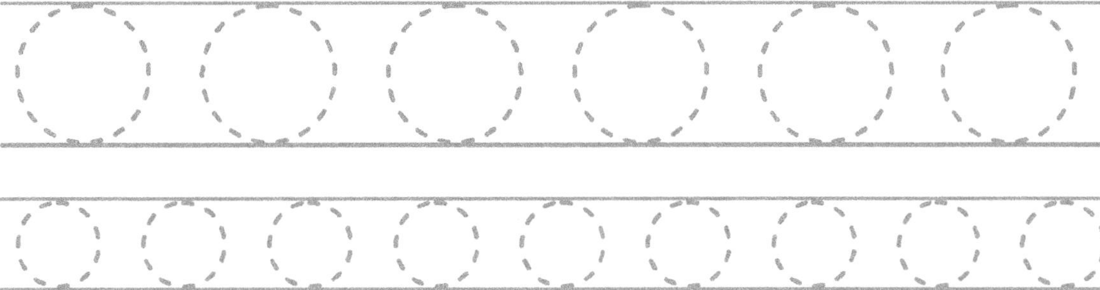

Find and color O:

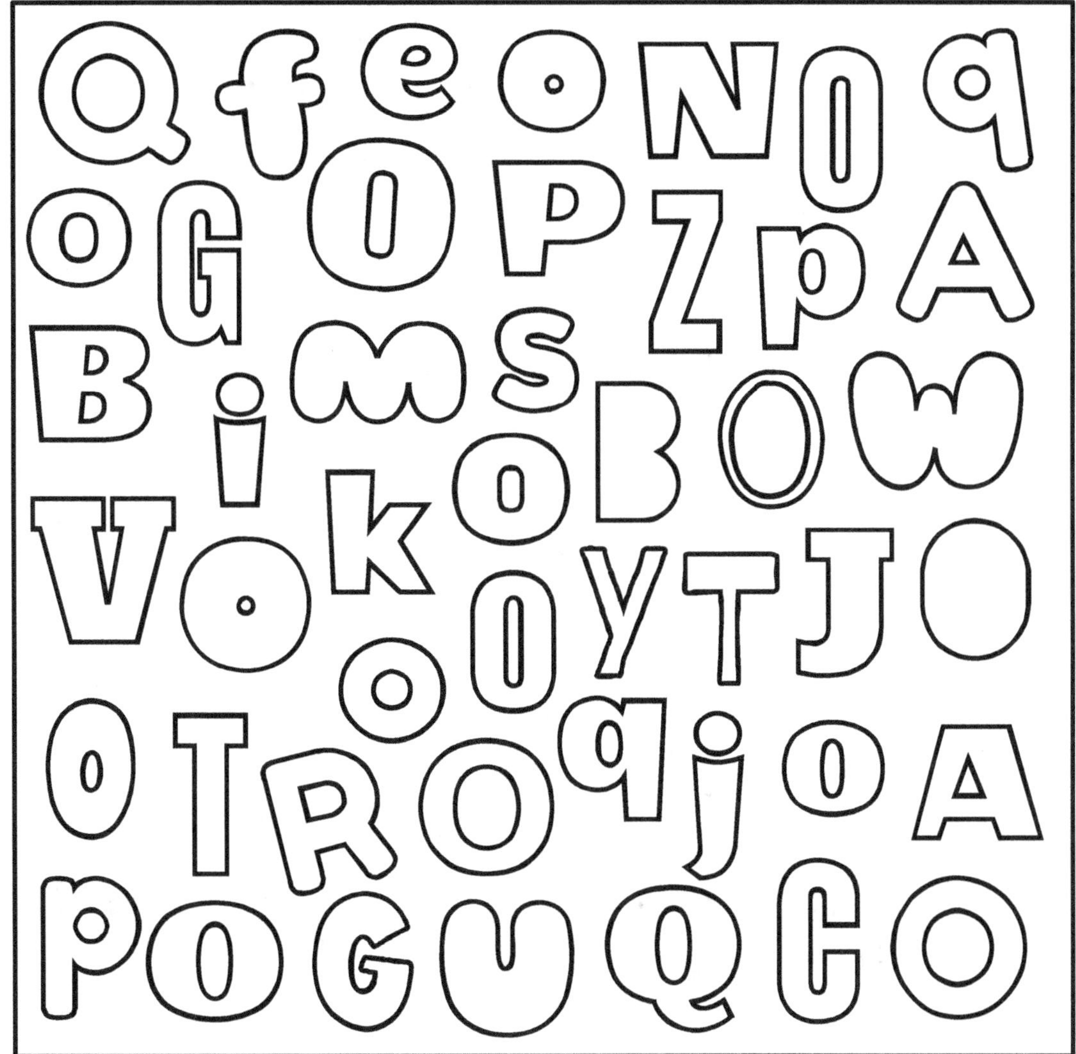

TRACE THE ALPHABET

Trace the cell completely, to reveal the letter P

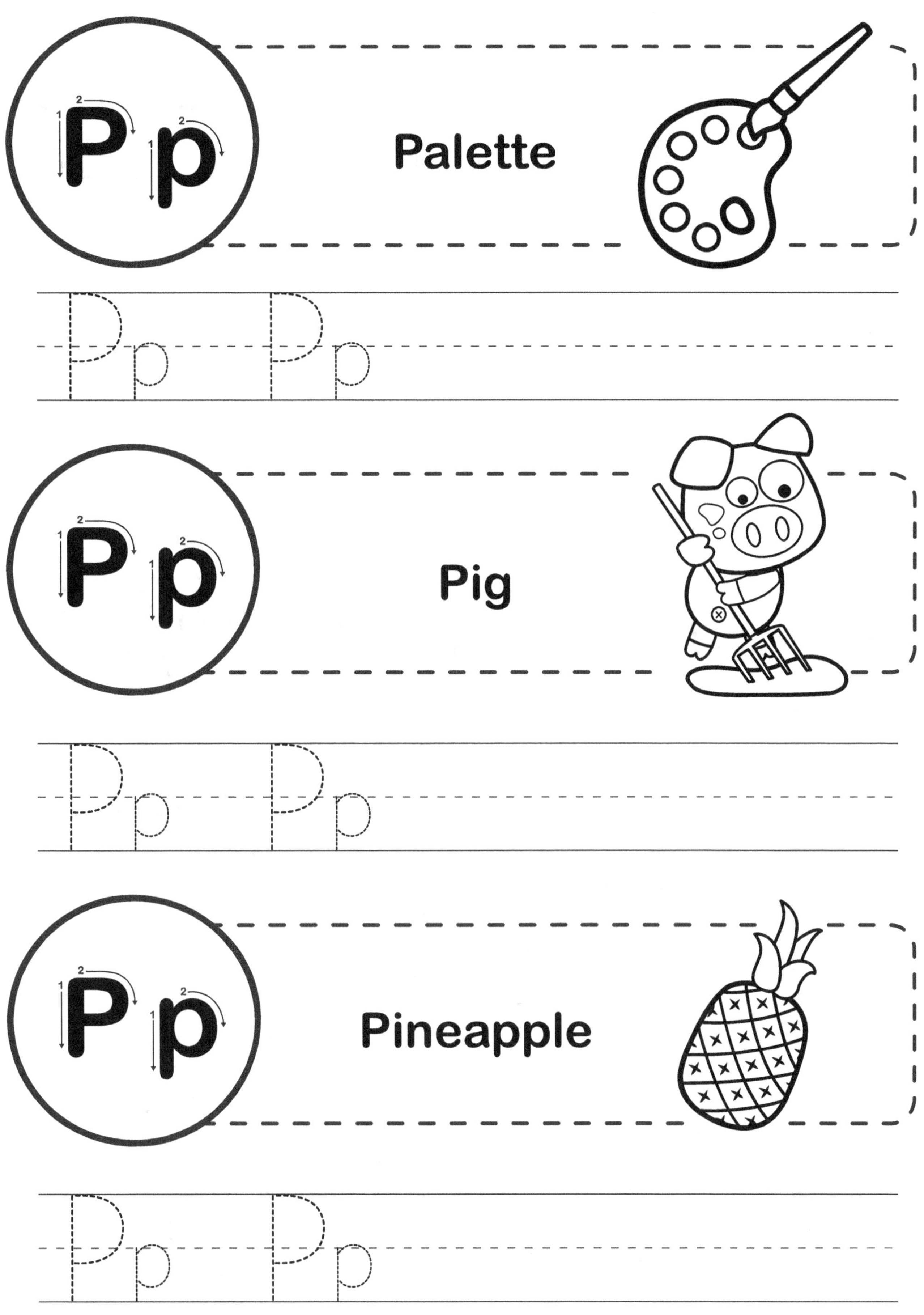
Palette
Pig
Pineapple

Name:

Date:

Trace:

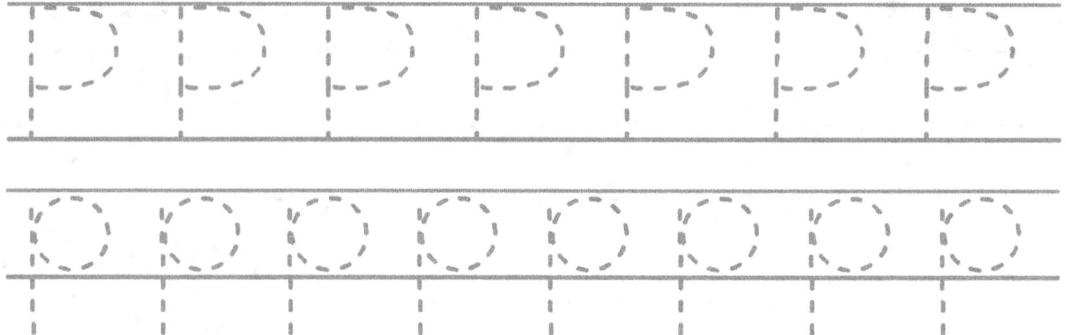

Find and color P:

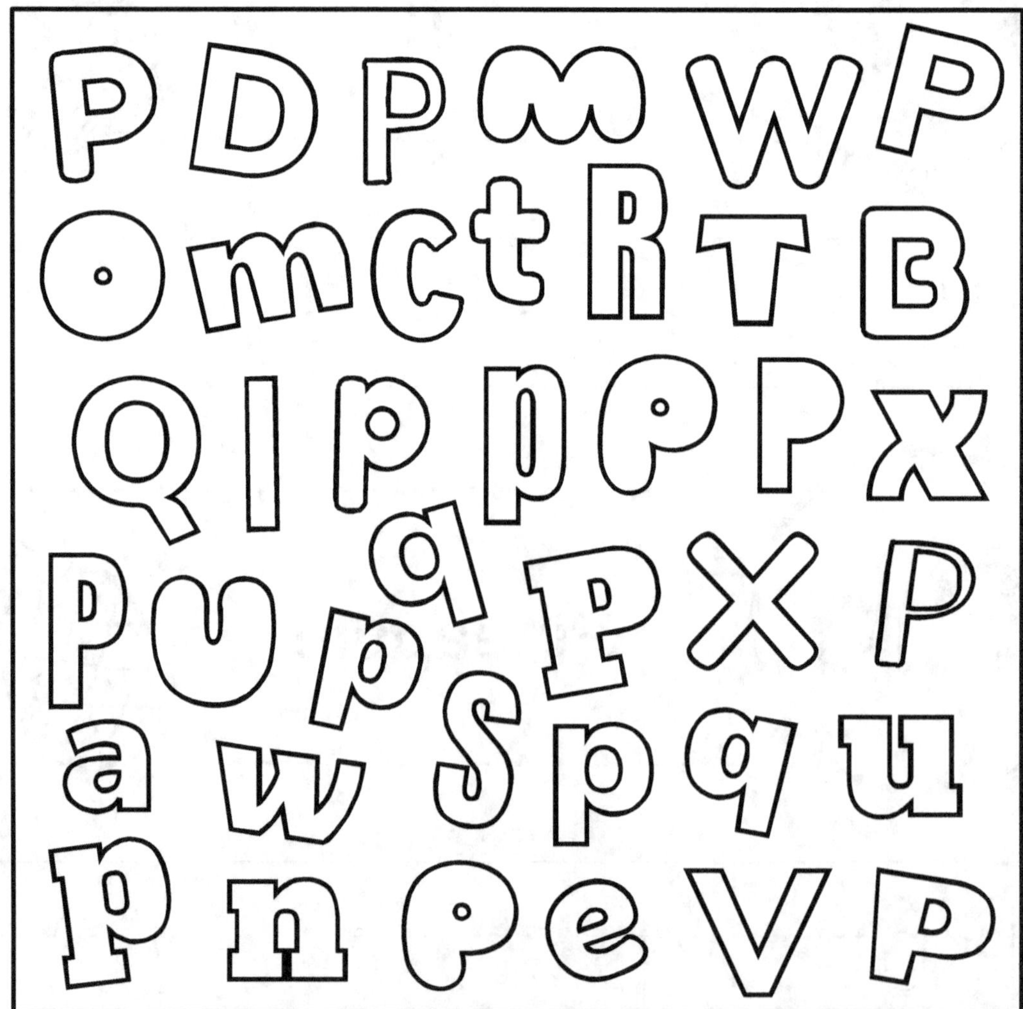

TRACE THE ALPHABET

Trace the cell completely, to reveal the letter Q

Q q
Quail
Q q
Quince
Q q
Quilt

Trace:

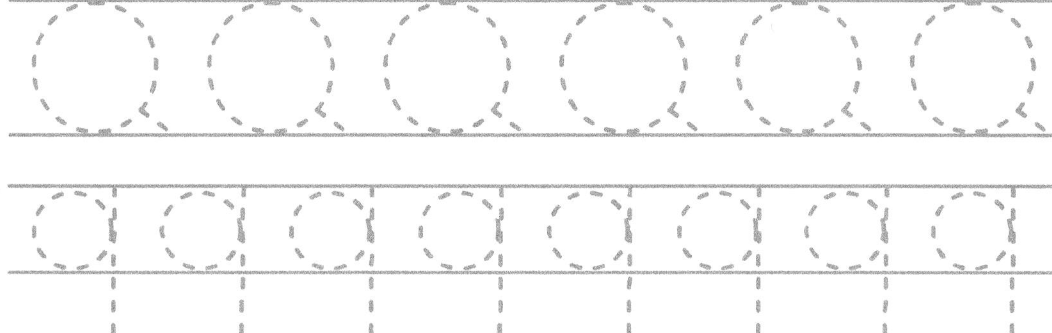

Find and color Q:

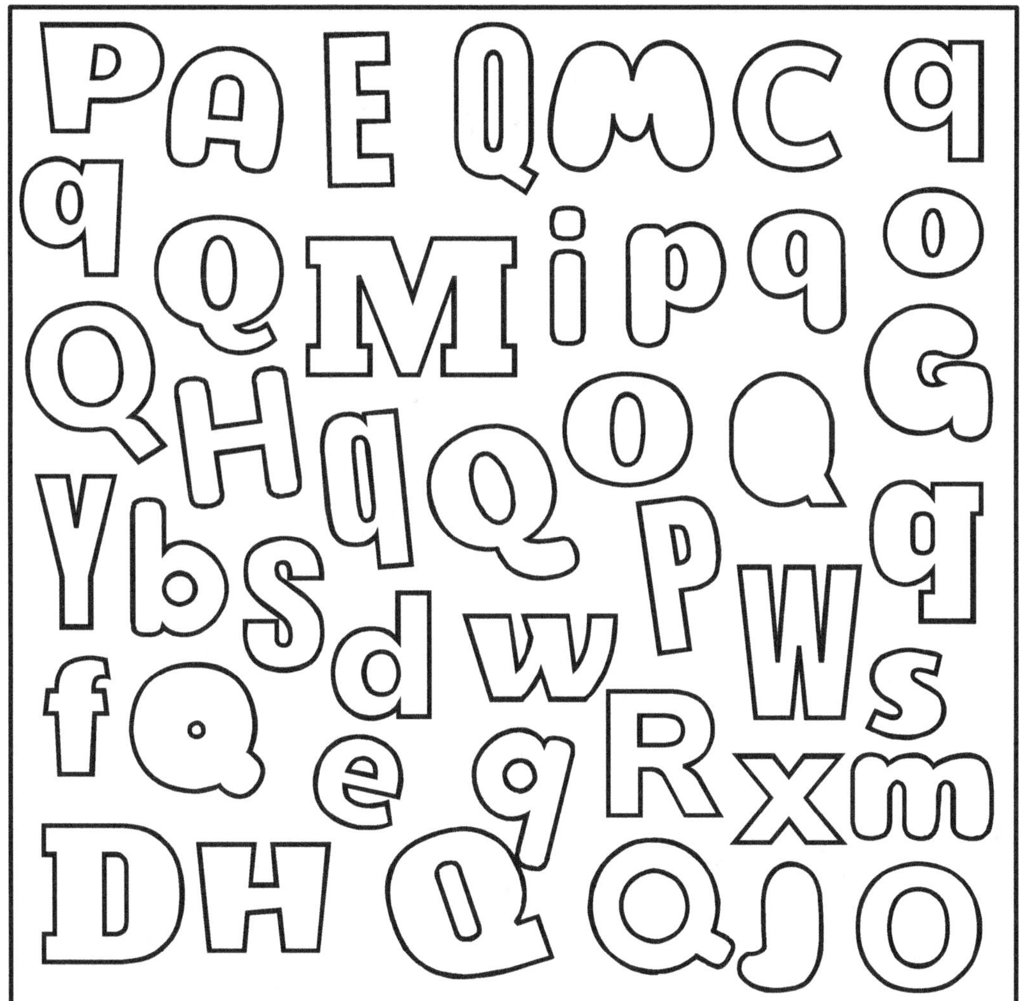

TRACE THE ALPHABET

Trace the cell completely, to reveal the letter R

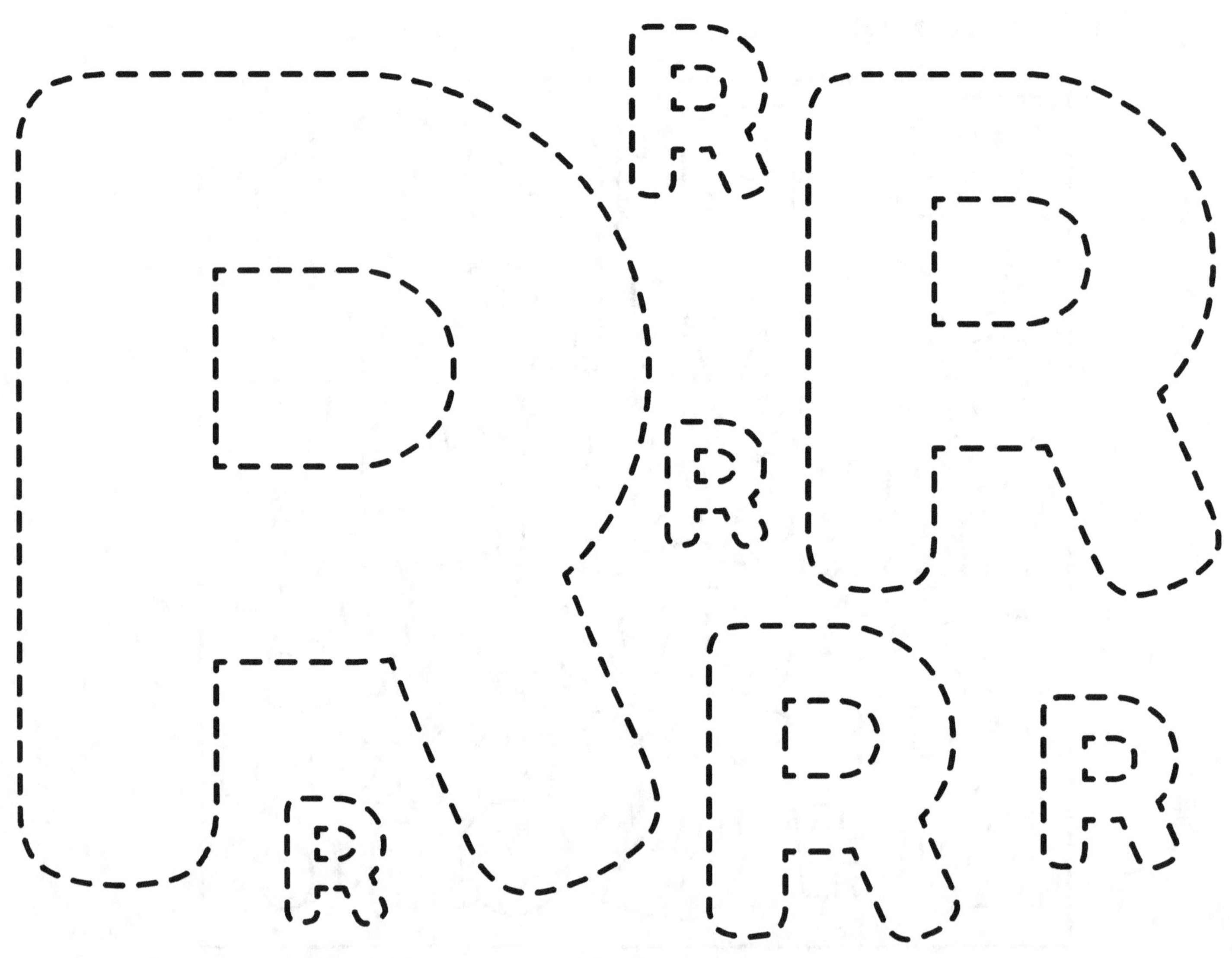

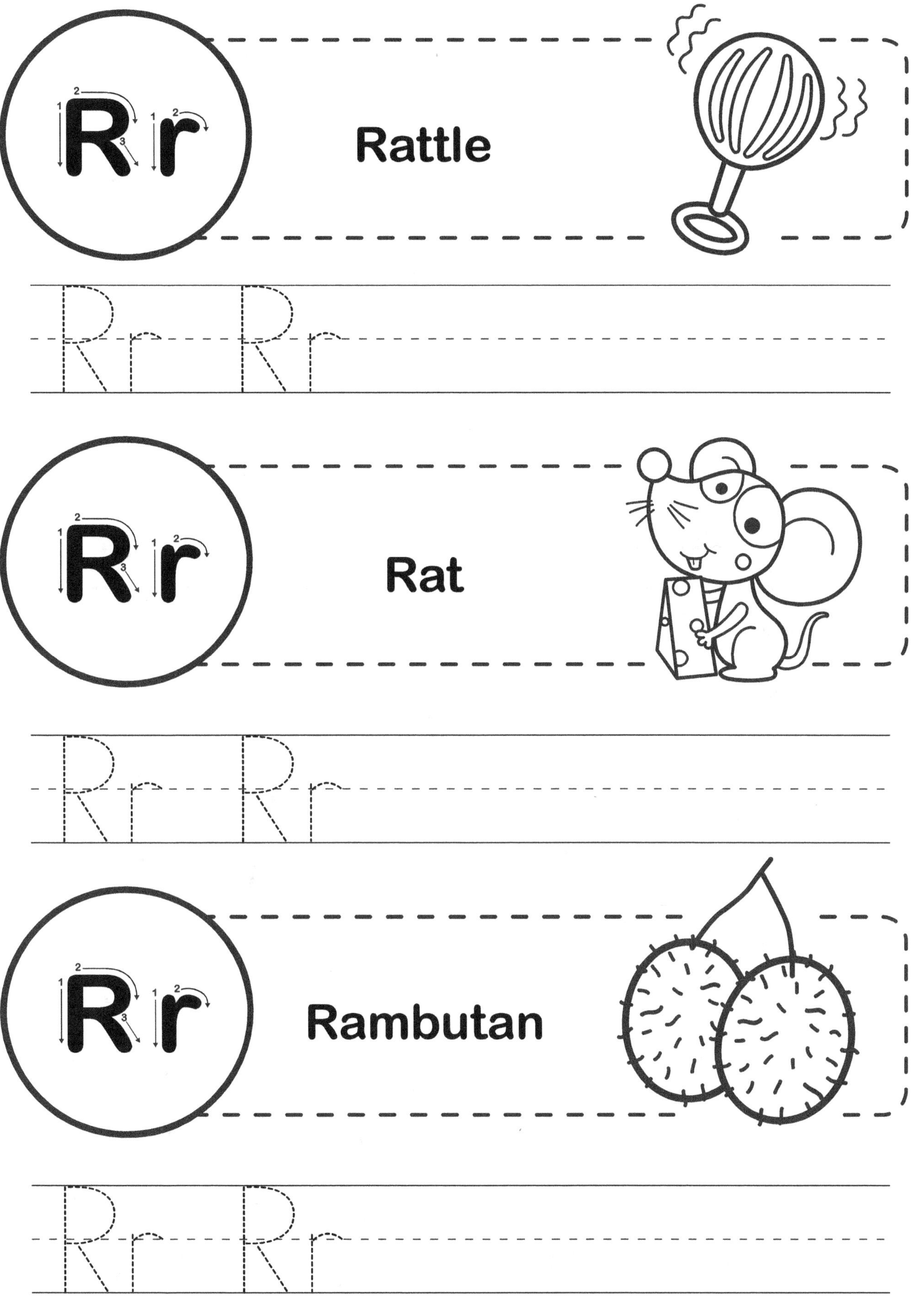

Rattle
Rat
Rambutan

Name:

Date:

Trace:

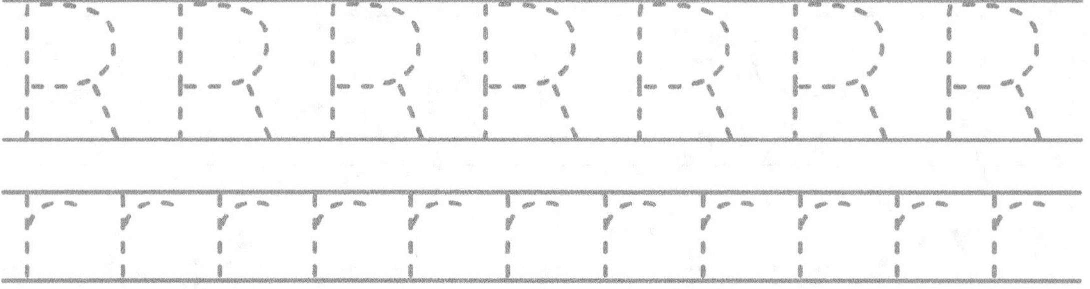

Find and color R:

TRACE THE ALPHABET

Trace the cell completely, to reveal the letter S

Star

Snake

Strawberry

Name:

Date:

Trace:

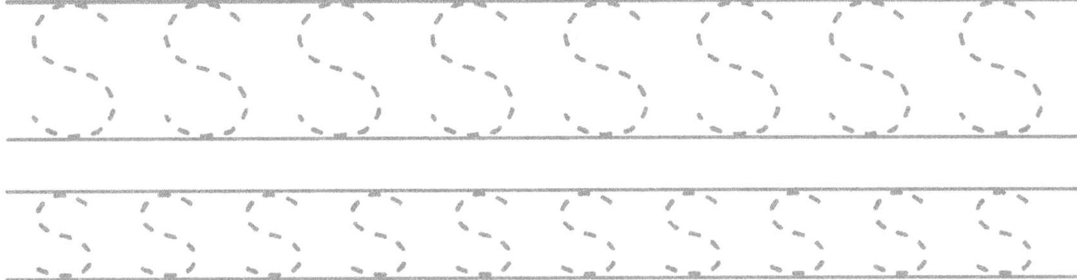

Find and color S:

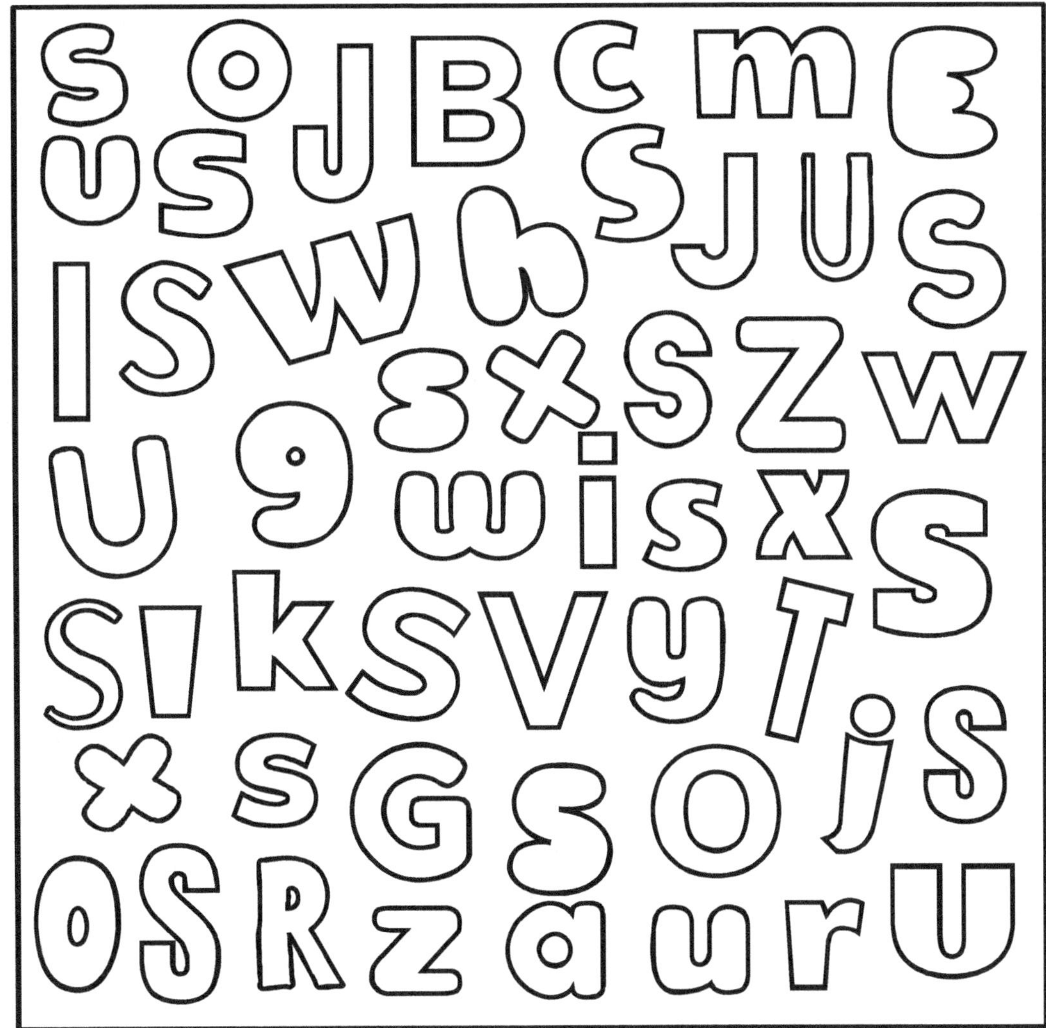

TRACE THE ALPHABET

Trace the cell completely, to reveal the letter T

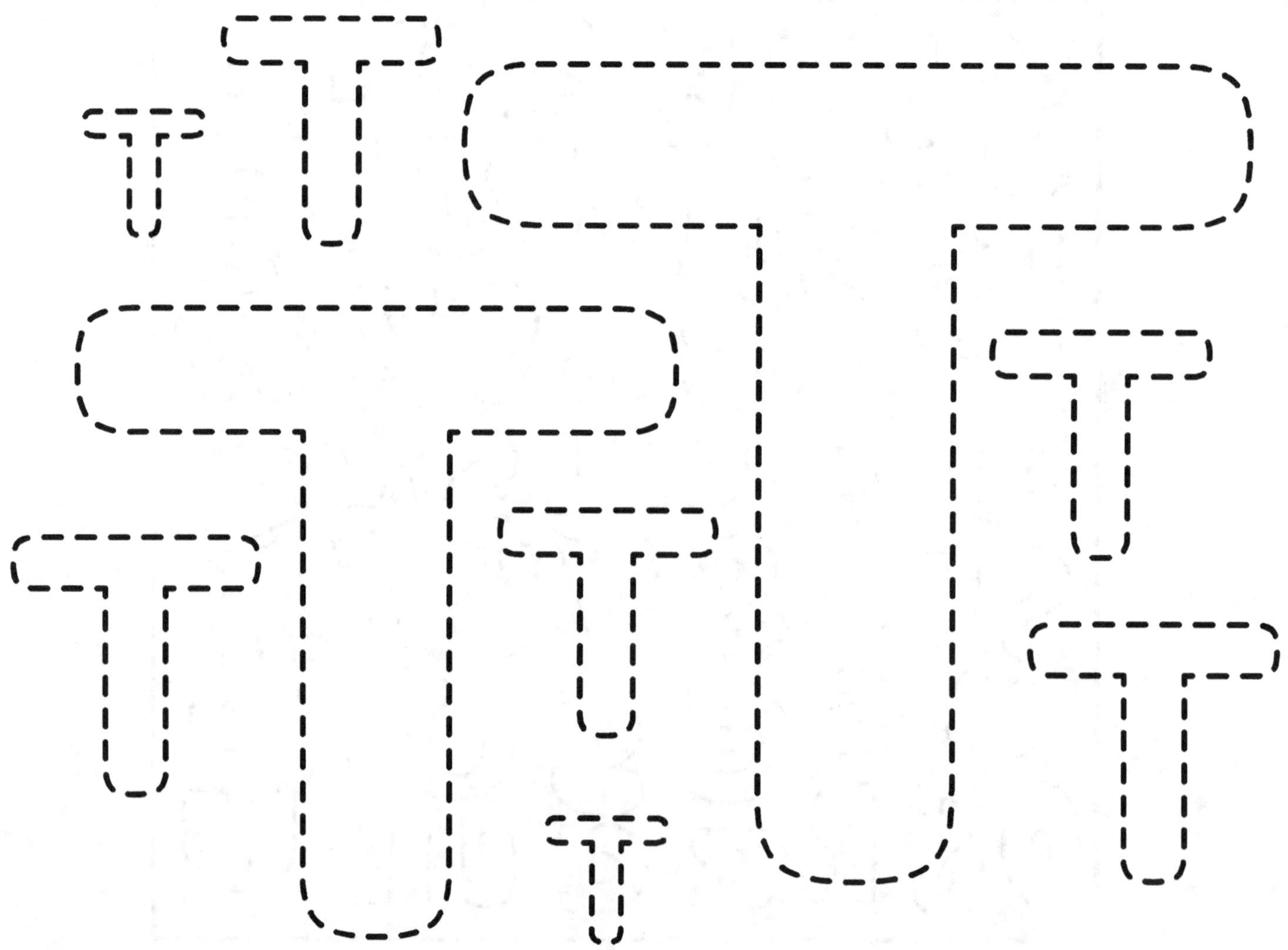

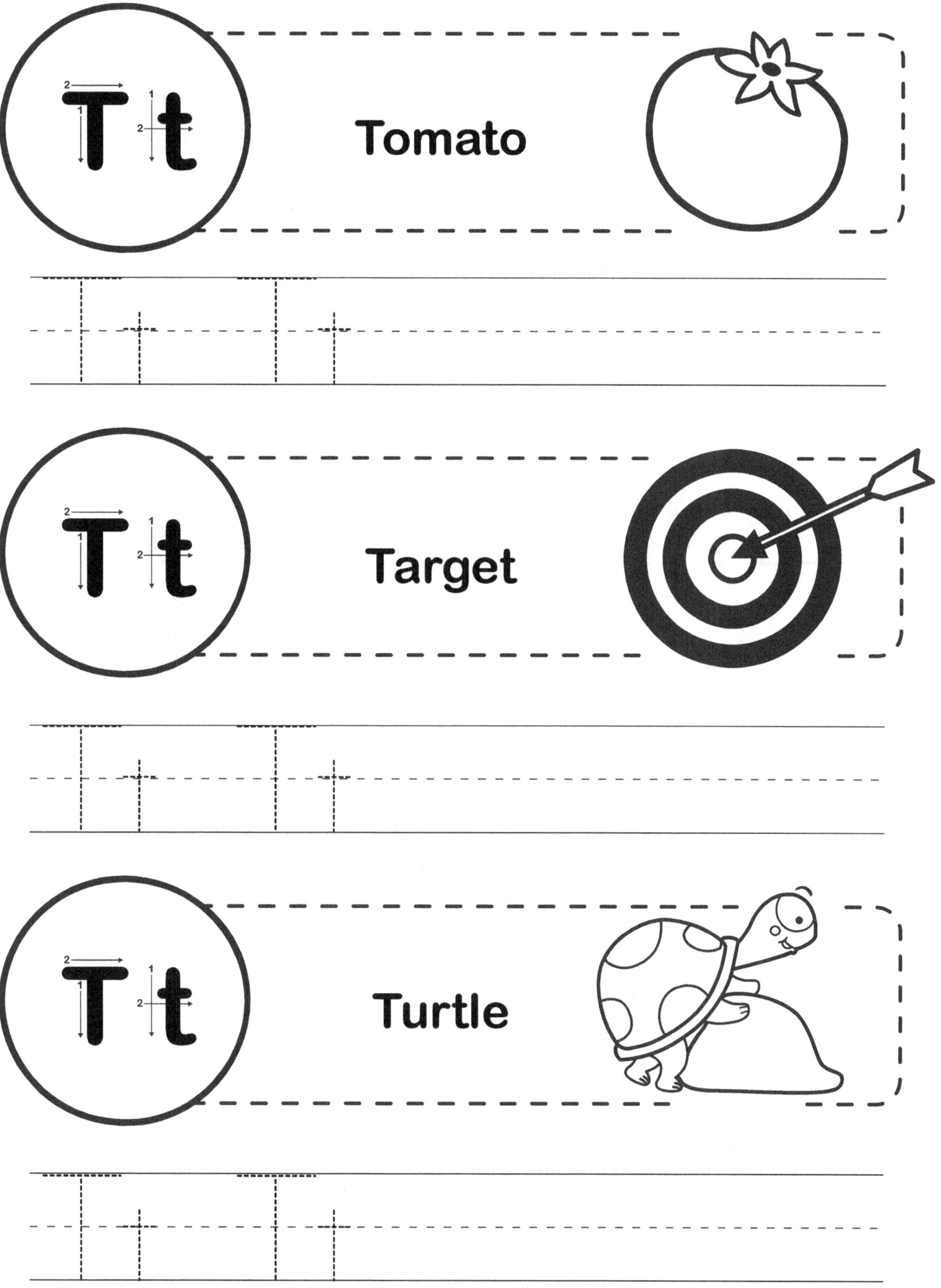

Tt

Tomato

Tt

Target

Tt

Turtle

Name:

Date:

Trace:

Find and color T:

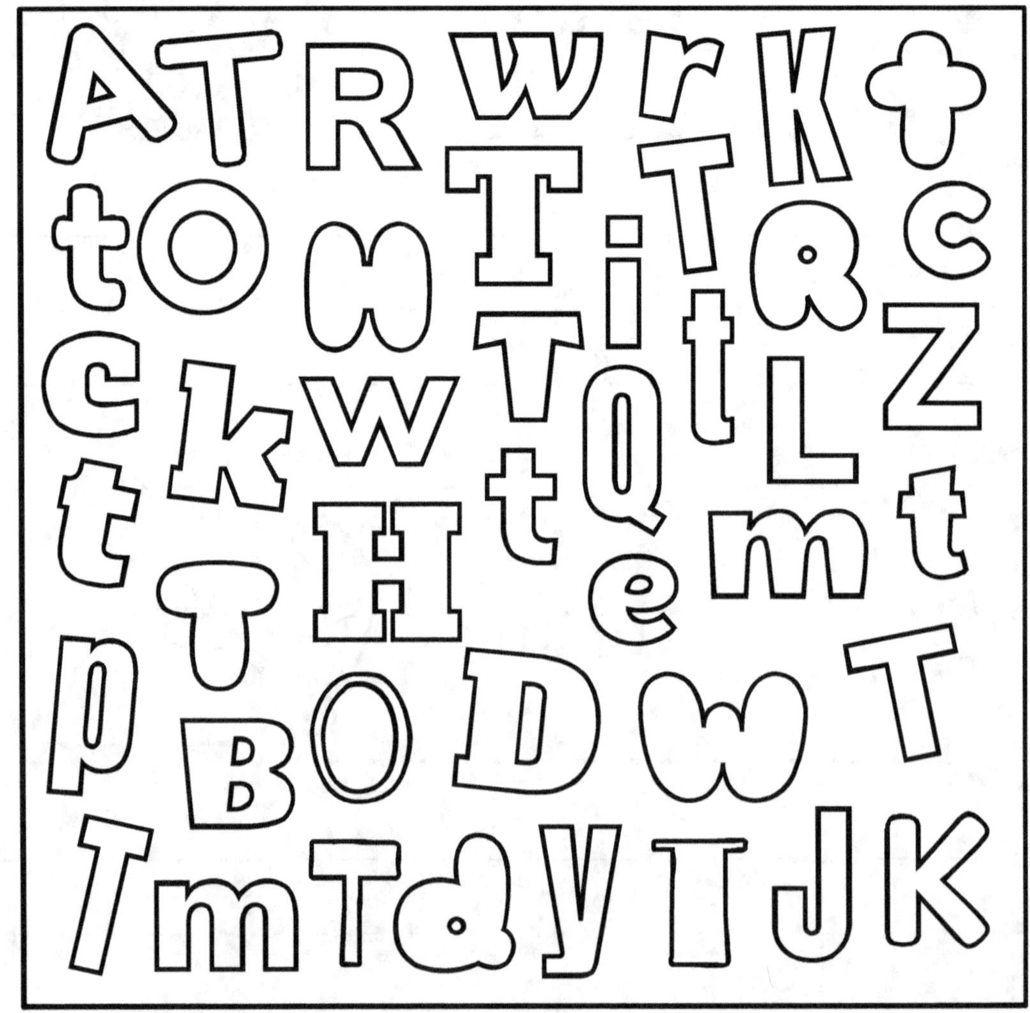

TRACE THE ALPHABET

Trace the cell completely, to reveal the letter U

Unicycle

Unicorn

Ugli fruit

Trace:

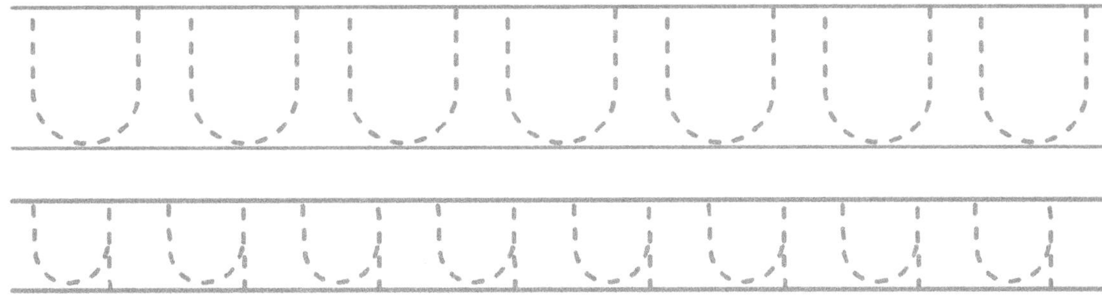

Find and color U:

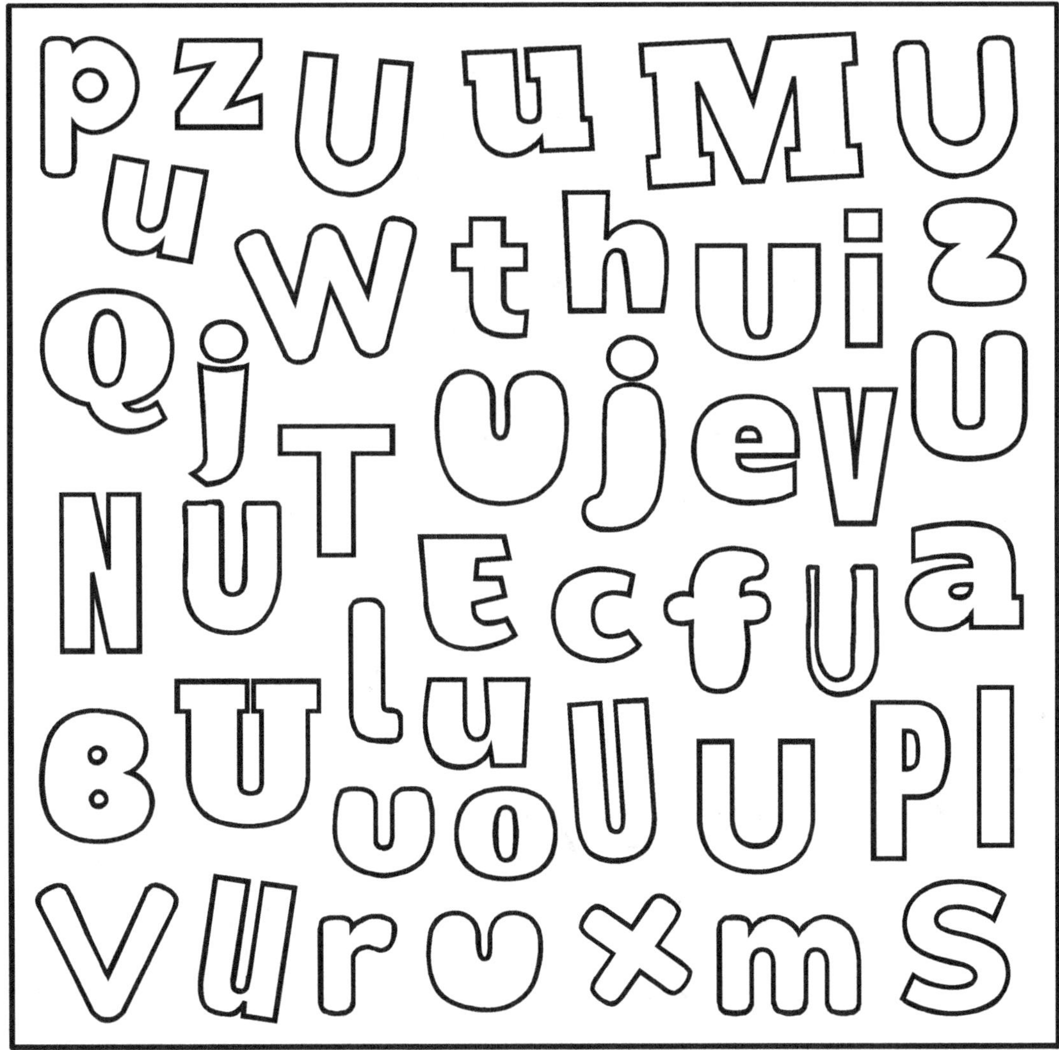

TRACE THE ALPHABET

Trace the cell completely, to reveal the letter V

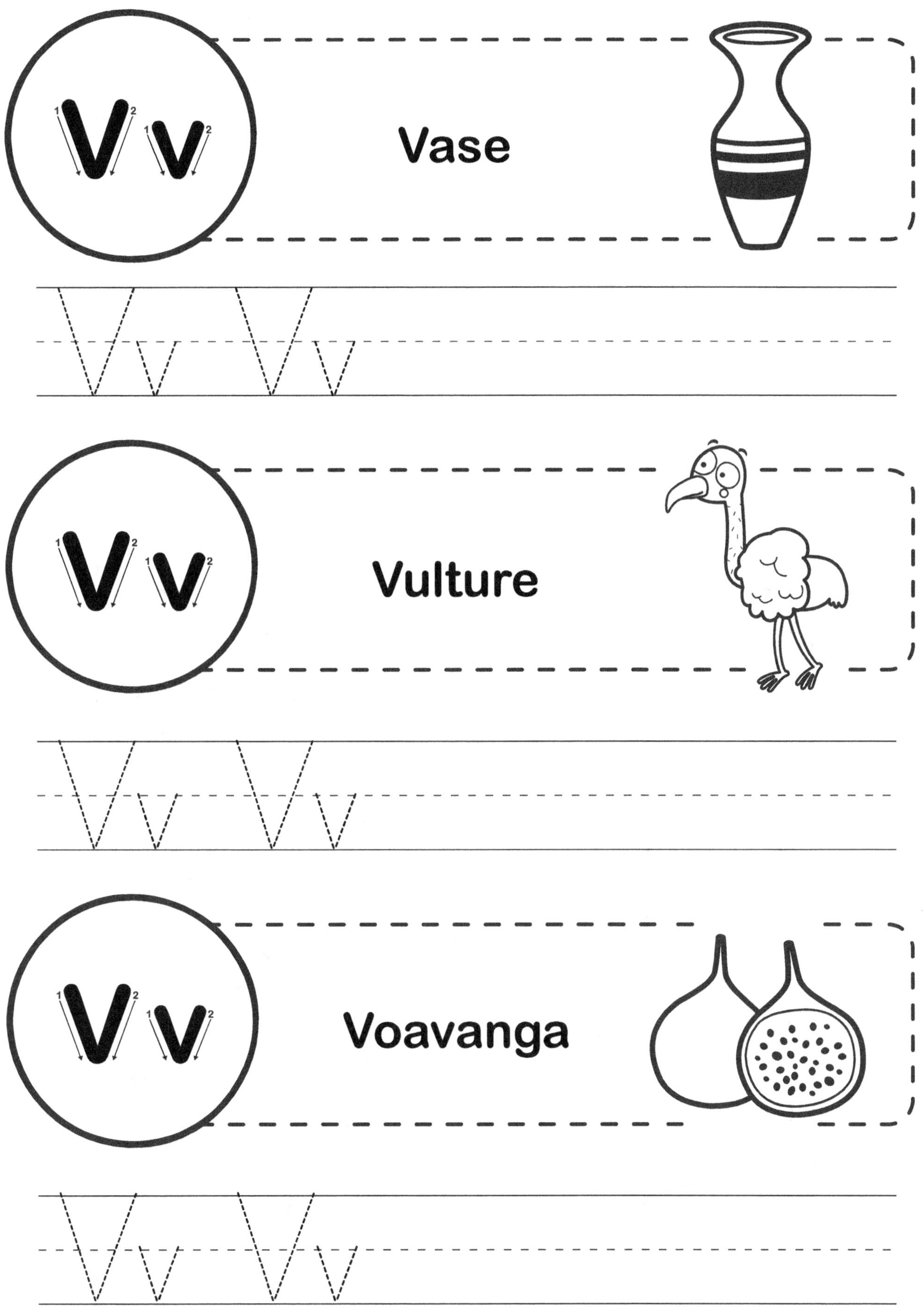

Vase

Vulture

Voavanga

Trace:

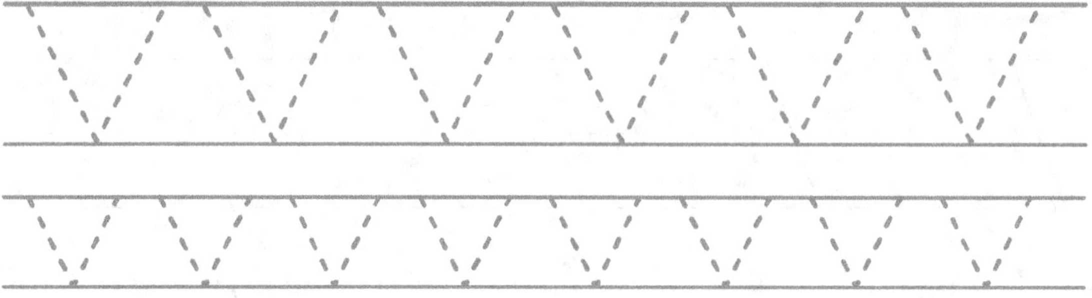

Find and color V:

TRACE THE ALPHABET

Trace the cell completely, to reveal the letter W

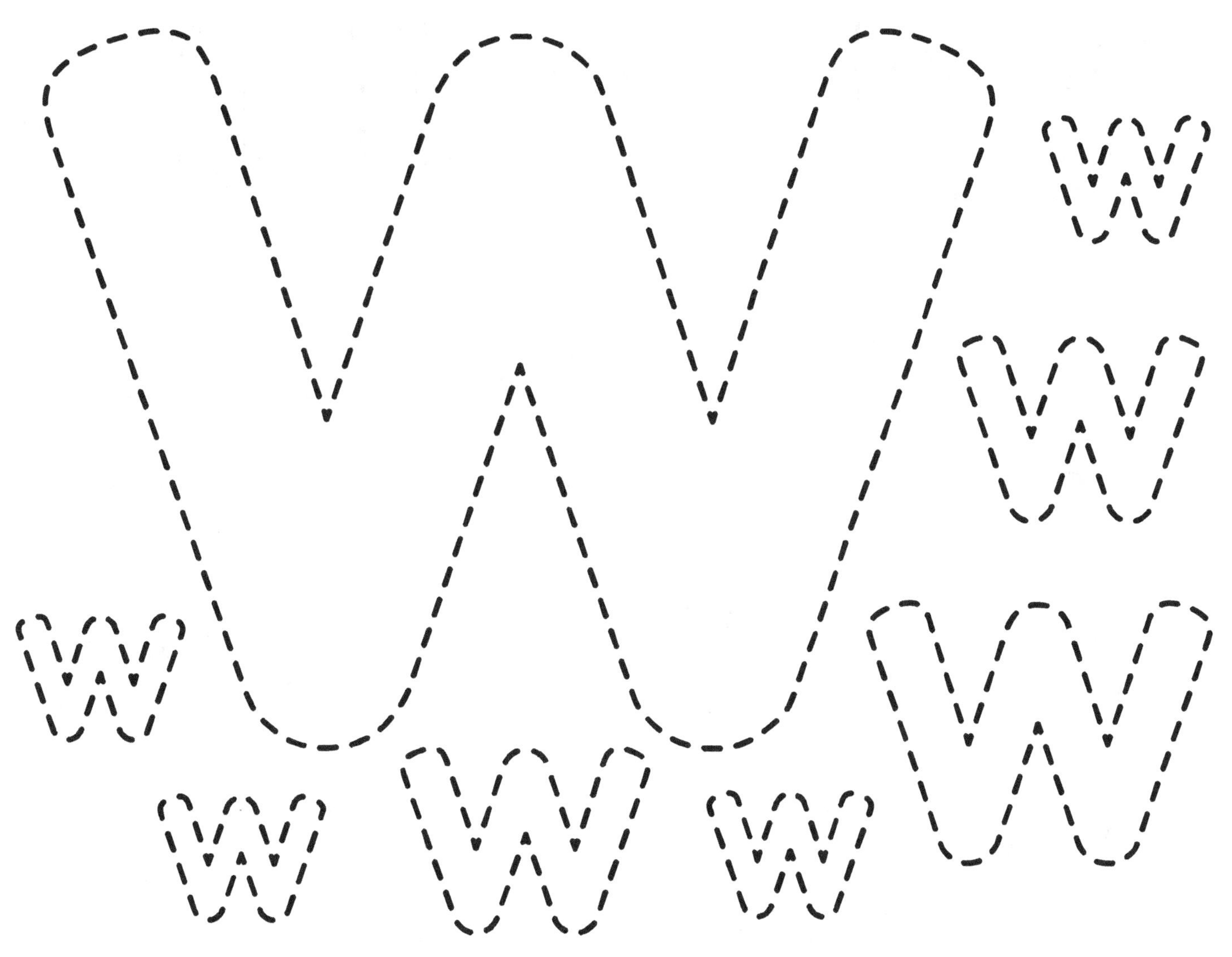

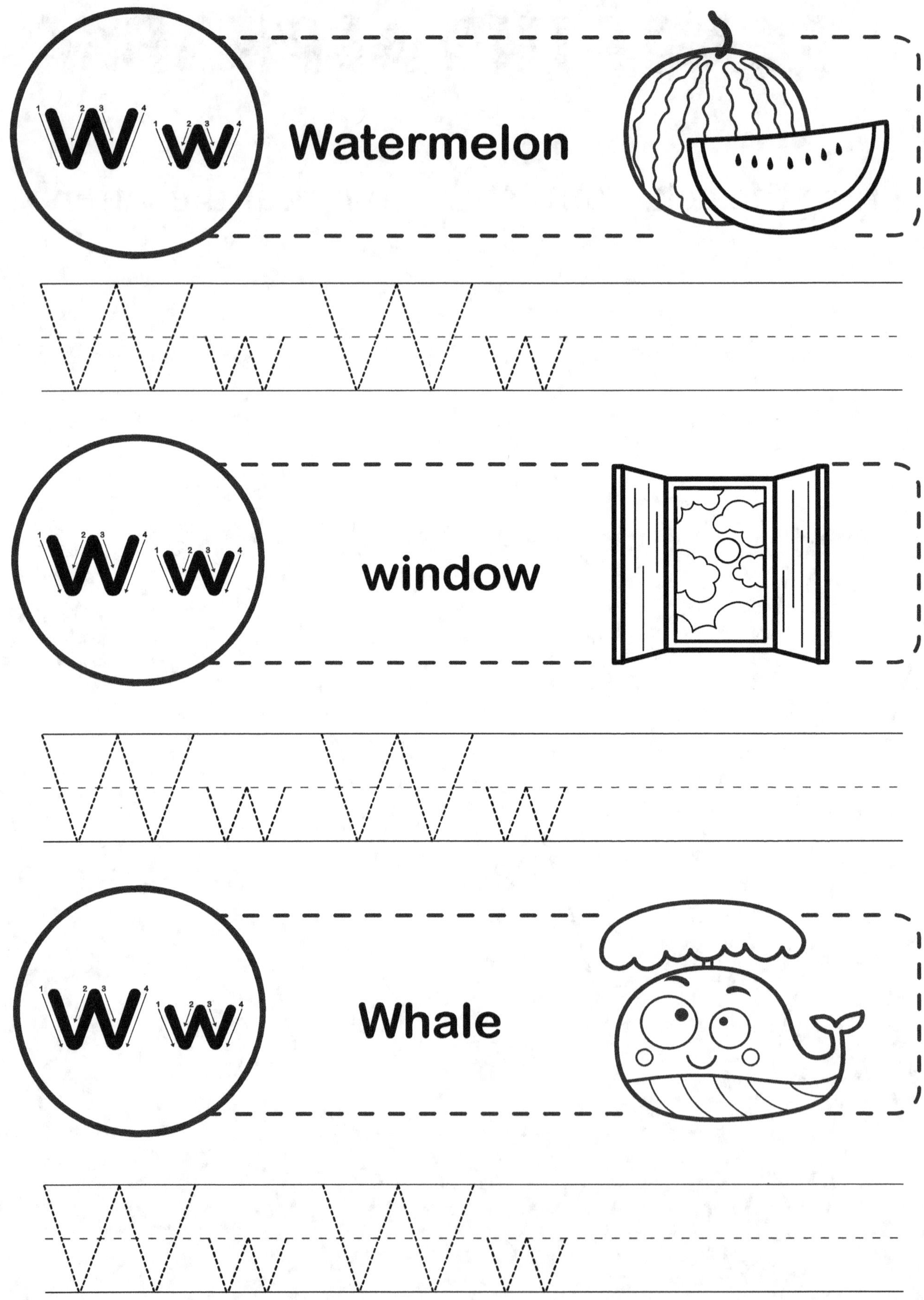

Watermelon

window

Whale

Trace:

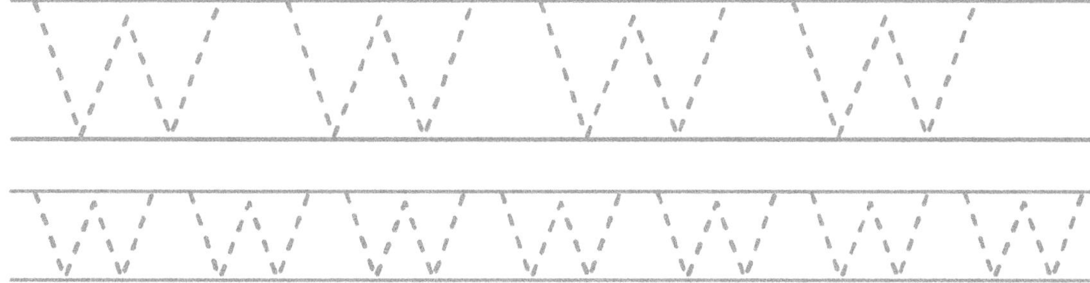

Find and color W:

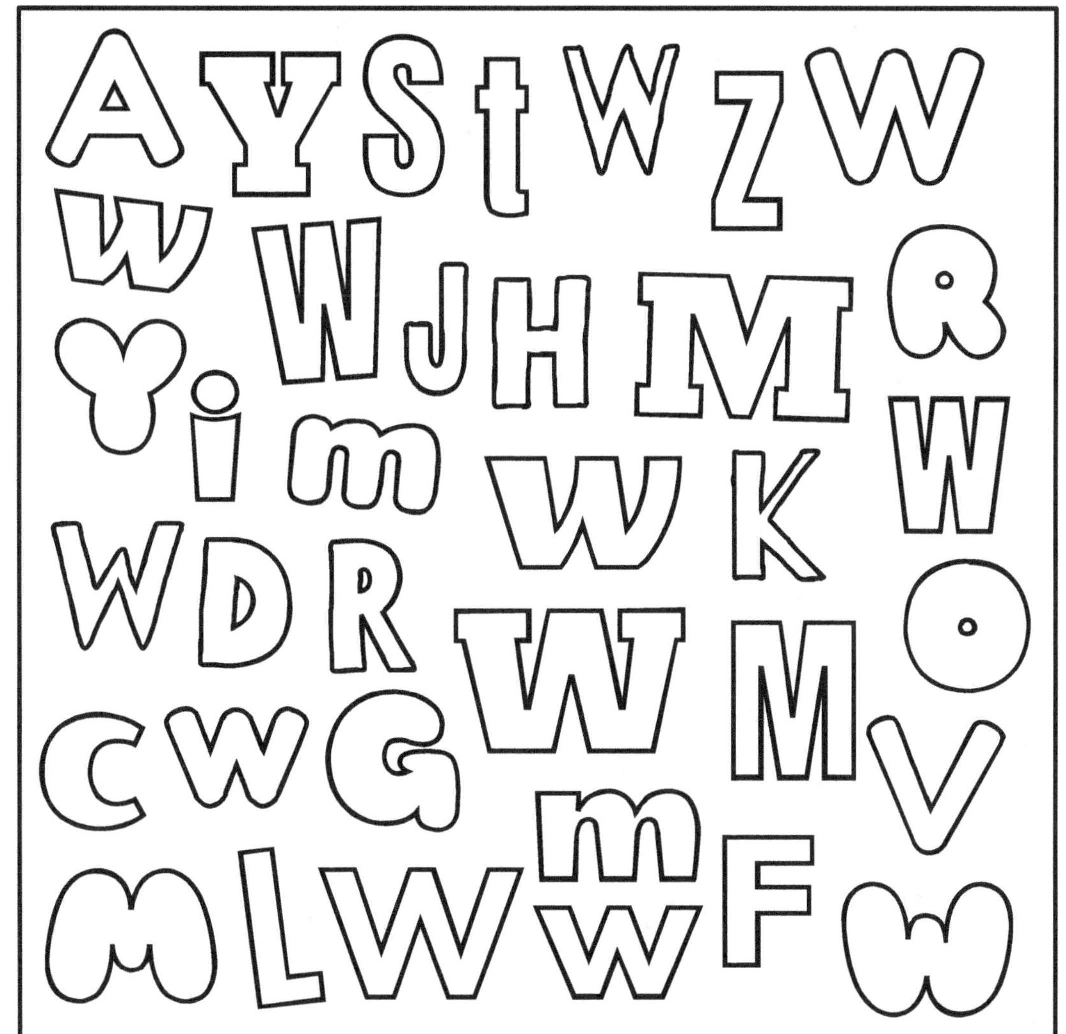

TRACE THE ALPHABET

Trace the cell completely, to reveal the letter X

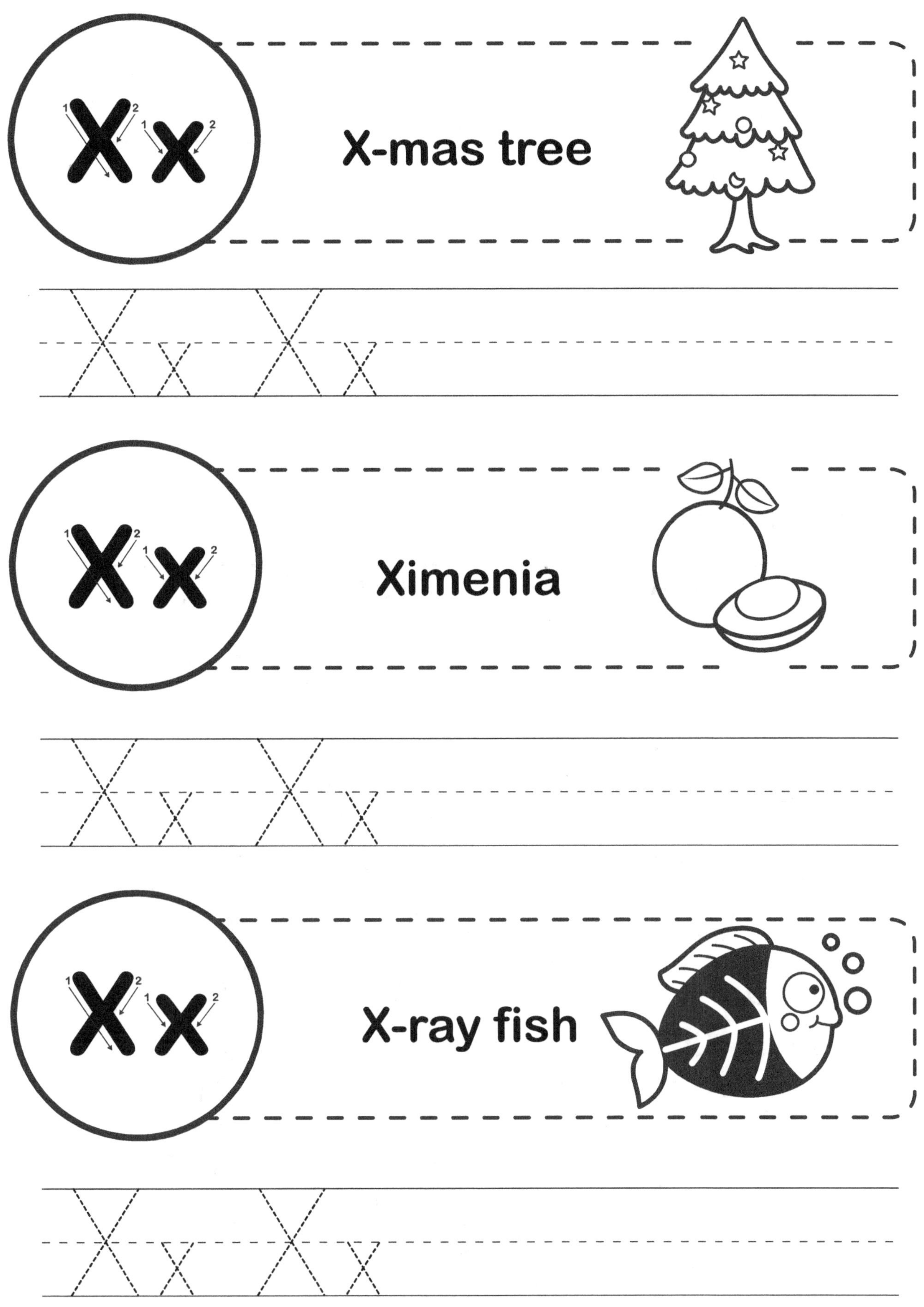

Xx
X-mas tree
Xx
Ximenia
Xx
X-ray fish

Trace:

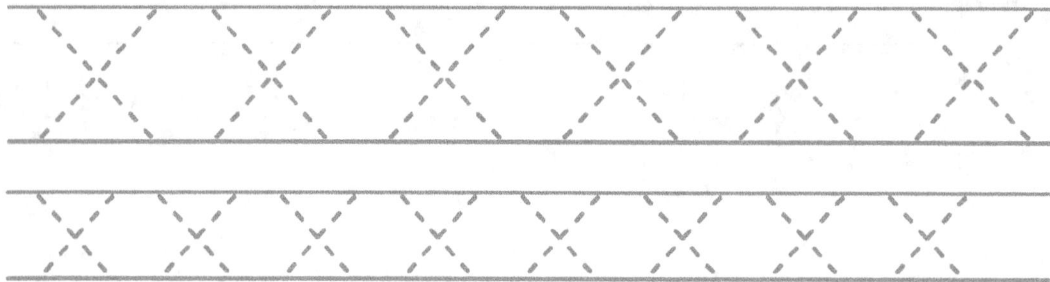

Find and color X:

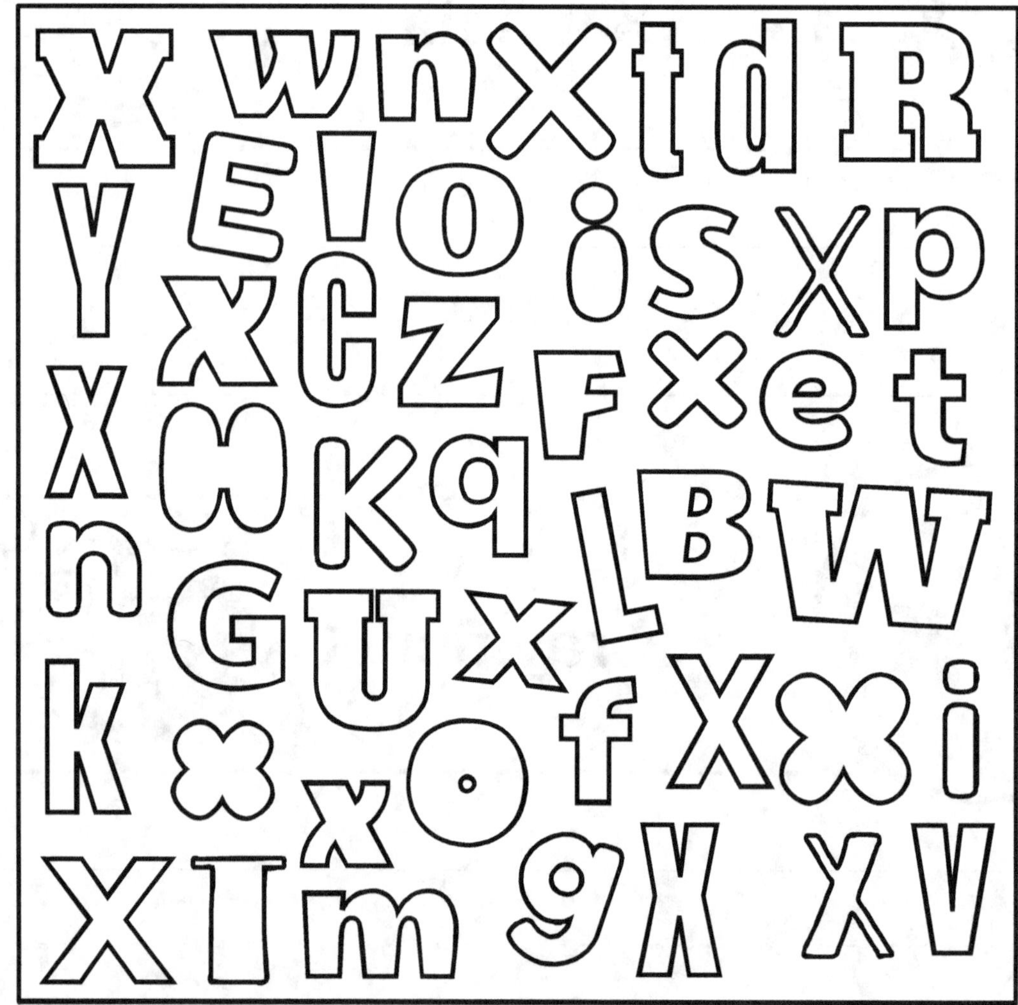

TRACE THE ALPHABET

Trace the cell completely, to reveal the letter Y

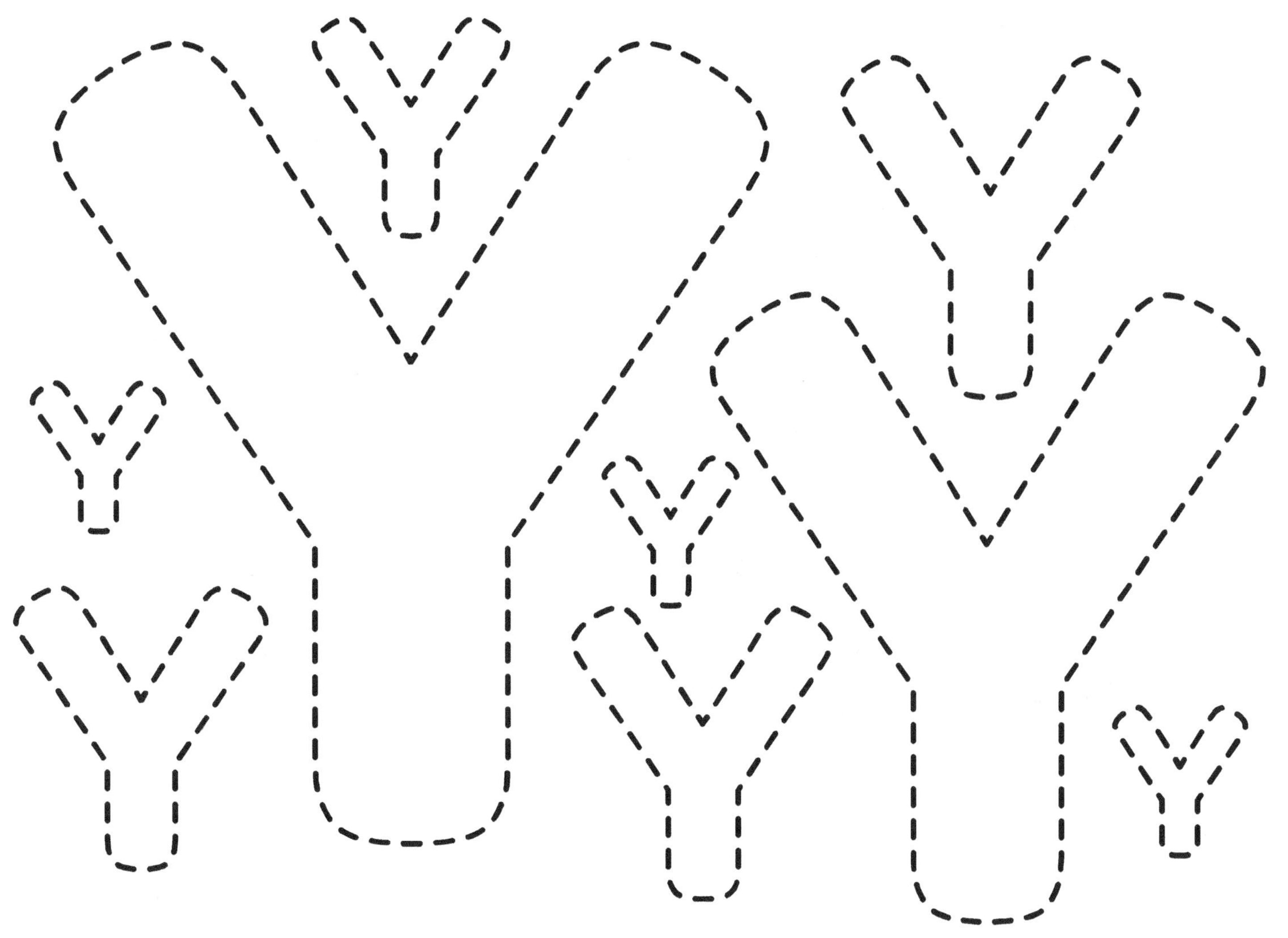

Yy
Yy
Yy
Yelk
Yak
Youngberry

Name:

Date:

Trace:

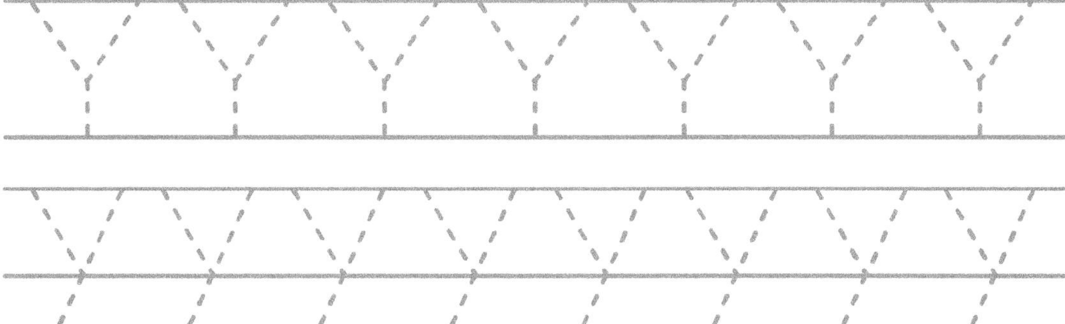

Find and color Y:

TRACE THE ALPHABET

Trace the cell completely, to reveal the letter Z

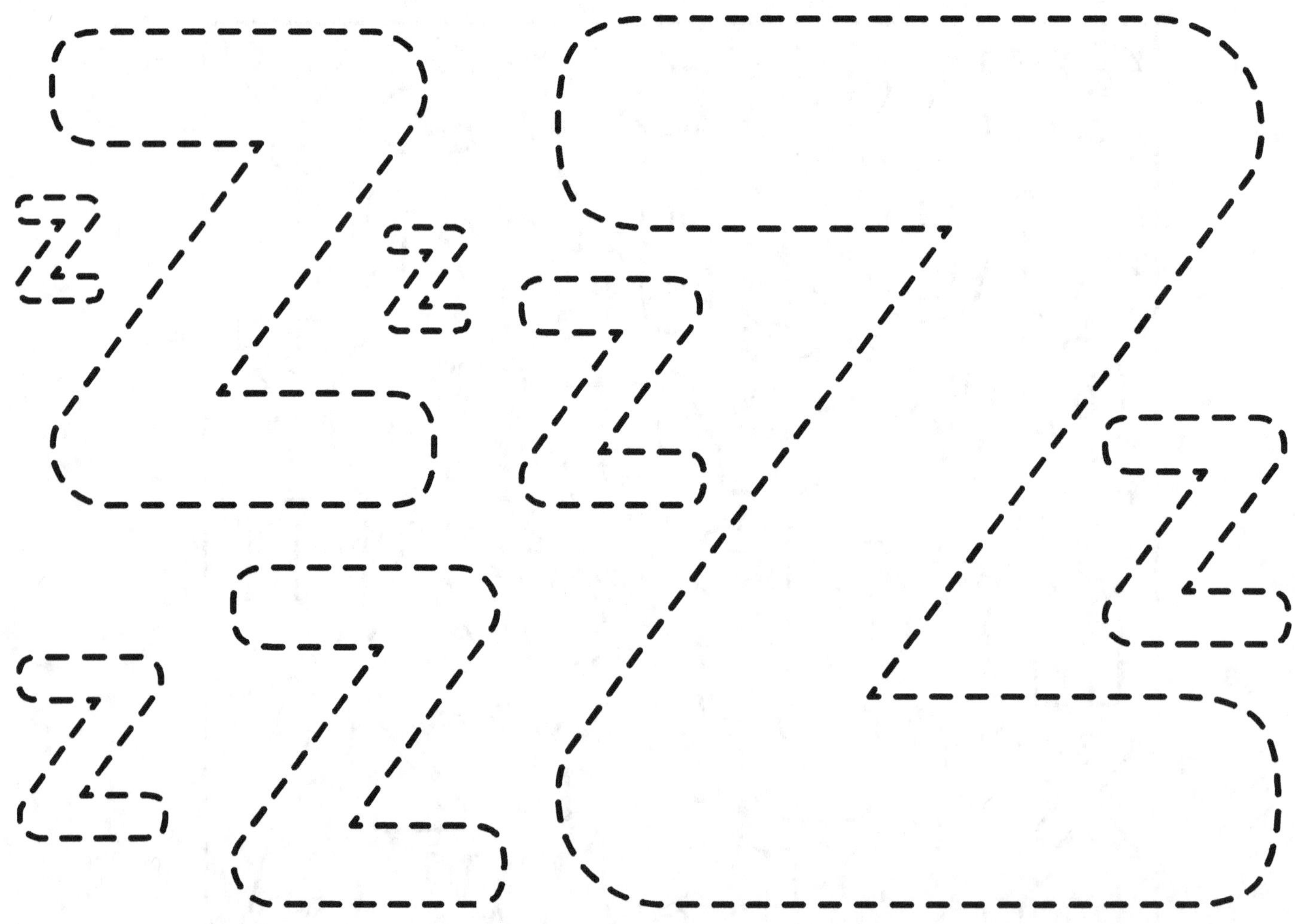

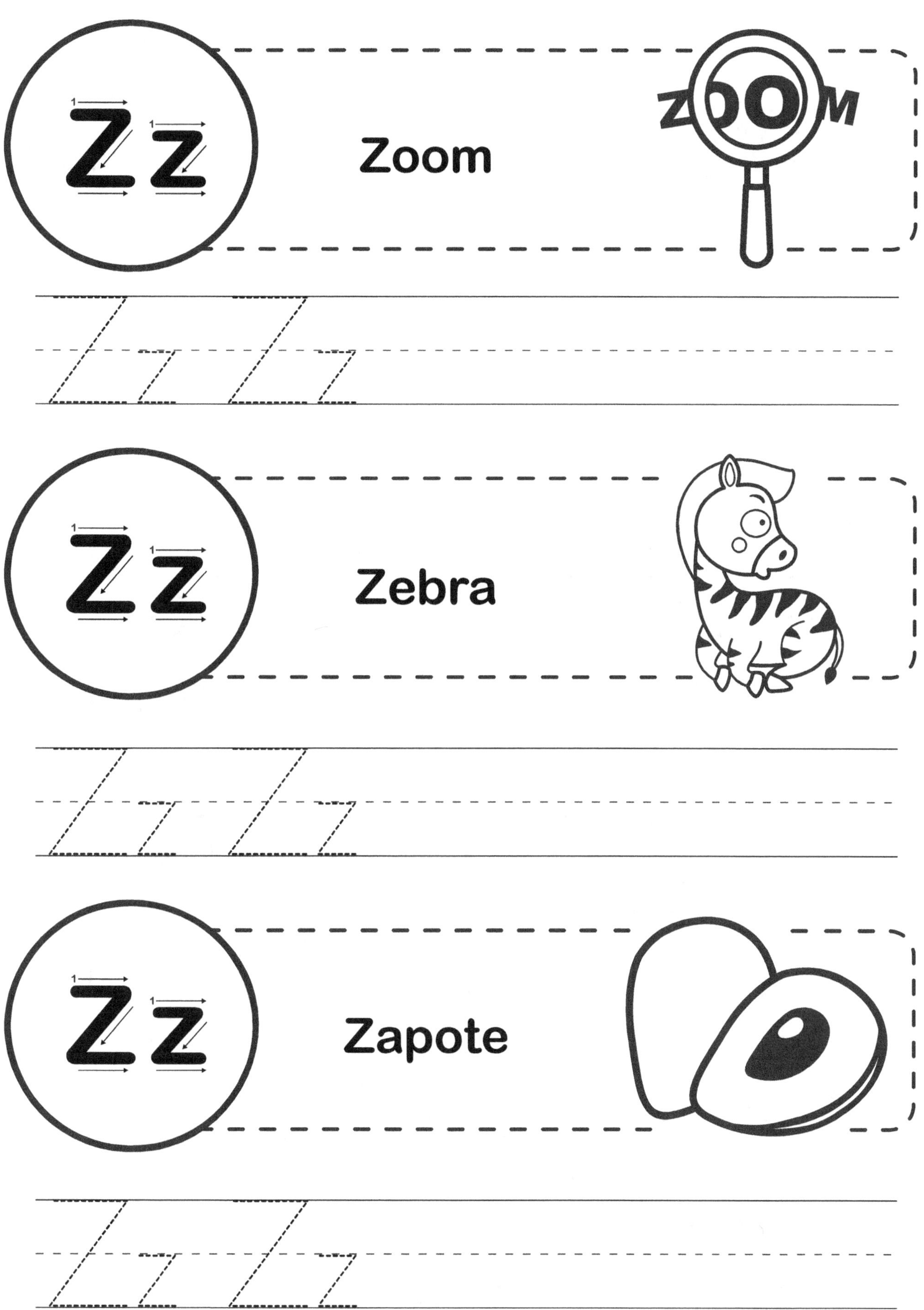

Zz
Zoom
Zz
Zebra
Zz
Zapote

Name:

Date:

Trace:

Find and color Z:

LET'S PRACTICE OUR NUMBER TRACING

TRACE THE NUMBER

Trace the cell completely, to reveal the number o

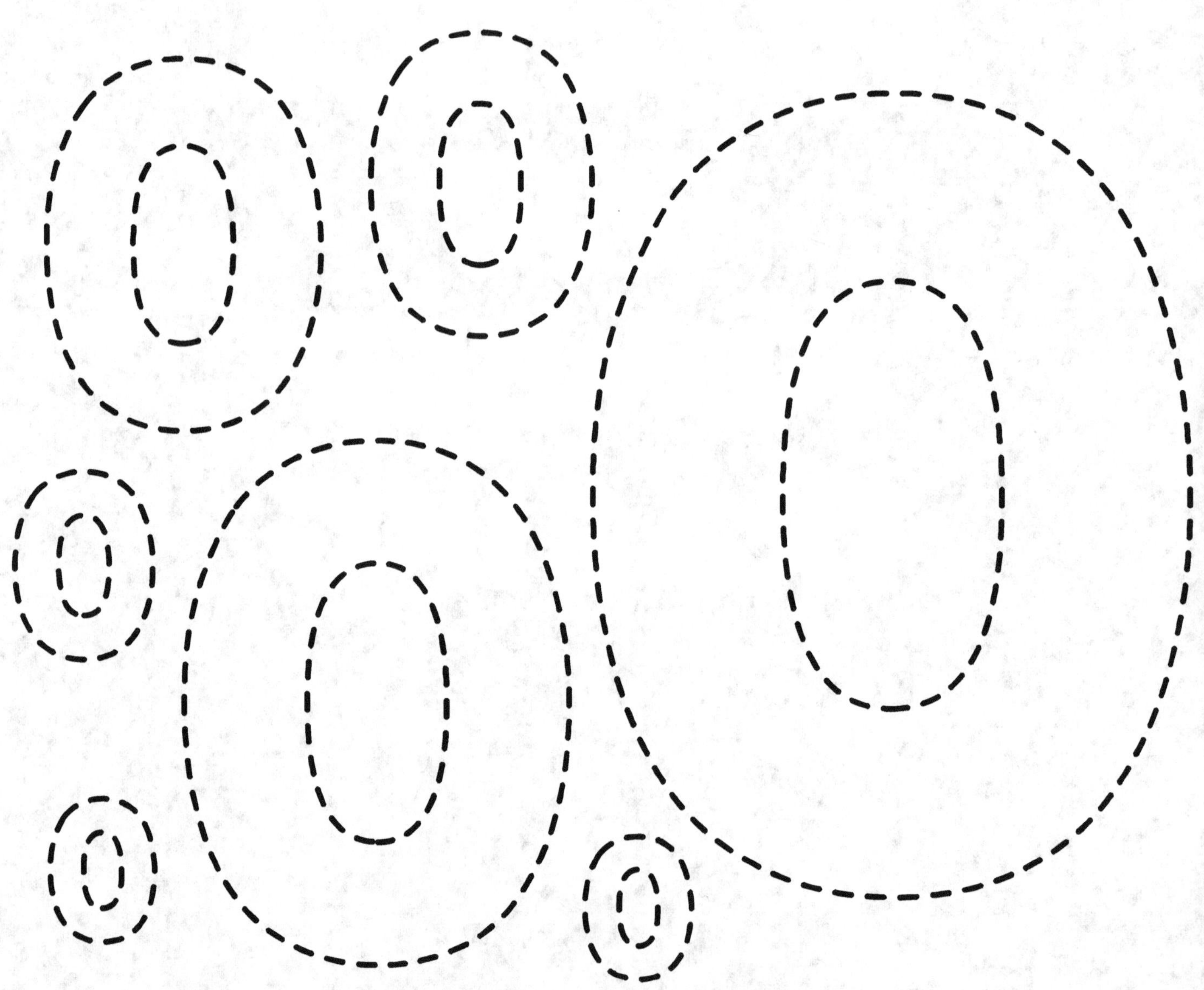

Trace:

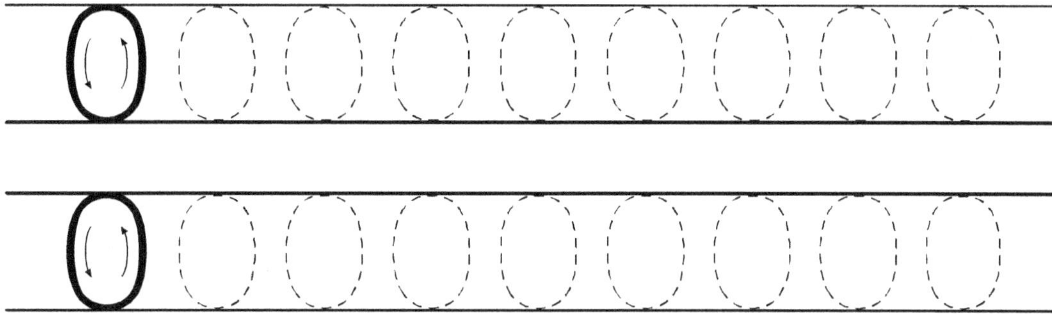

Find and color 0:

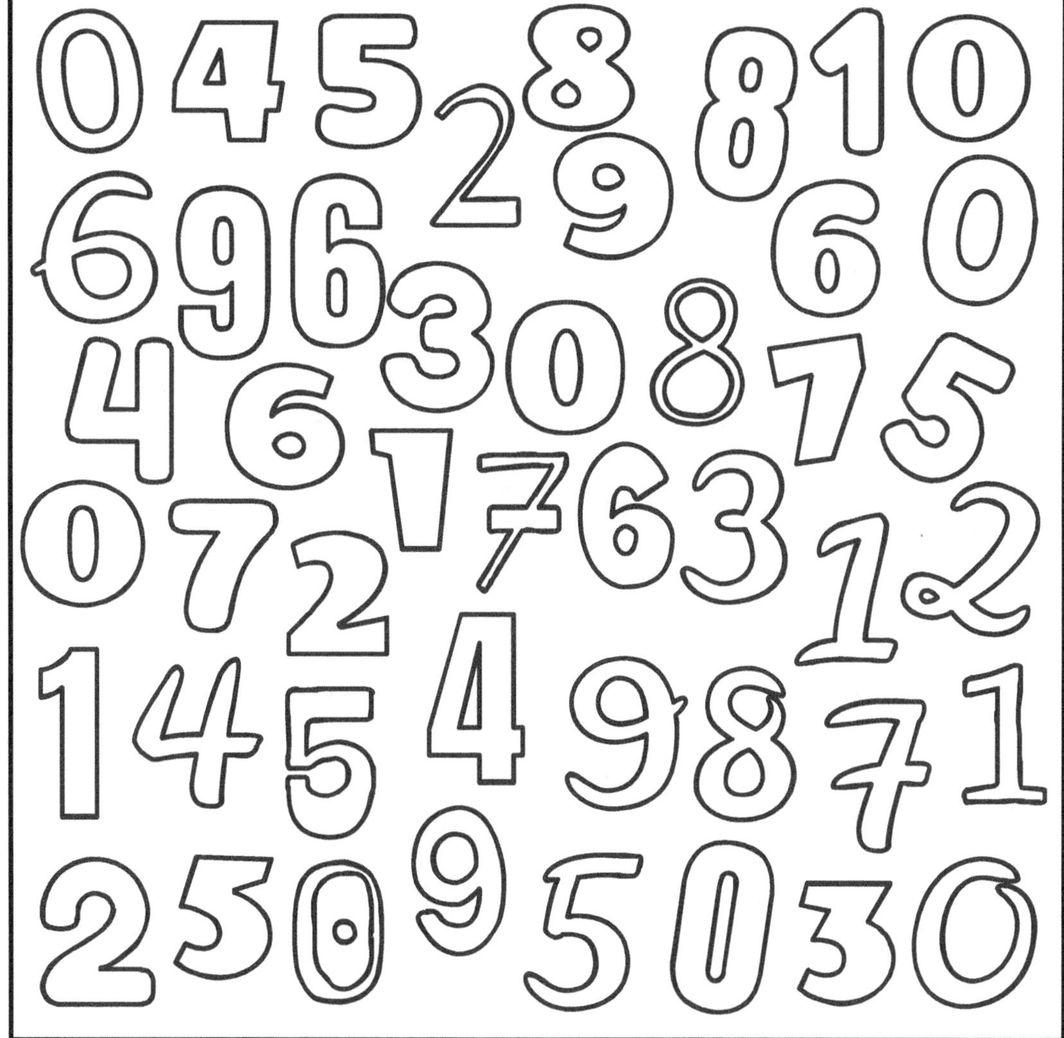

TRACE THE NUMBER

Trace the cell completely, to reveal the number 1

Trace:

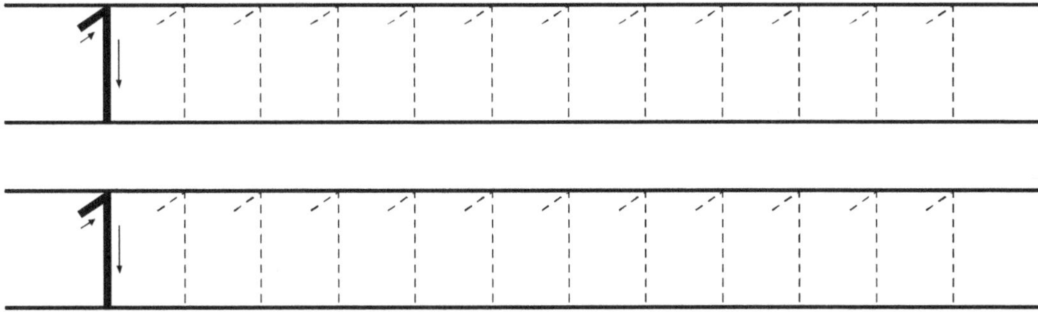

Find and color 1:

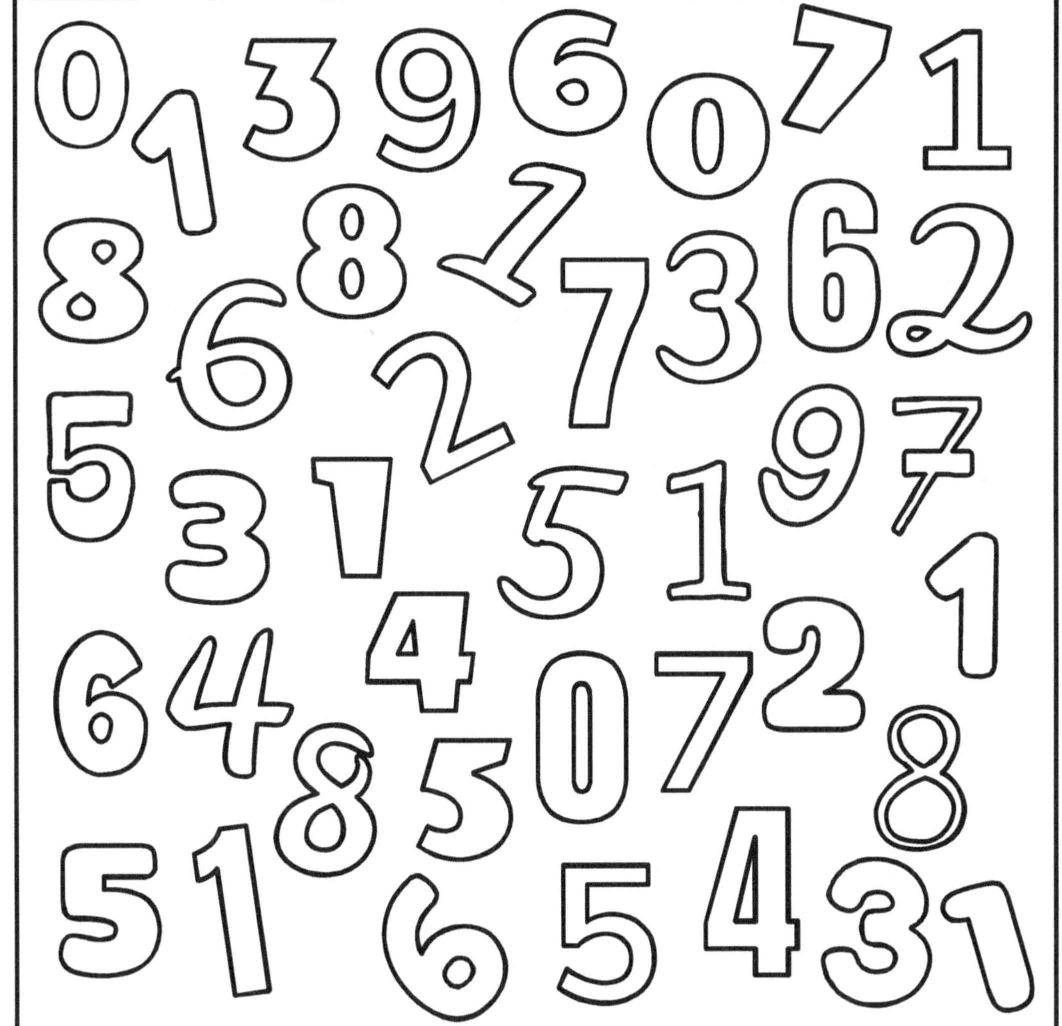

TRACE THE NUMBER

Trace the cell completely, to reveal the number 2

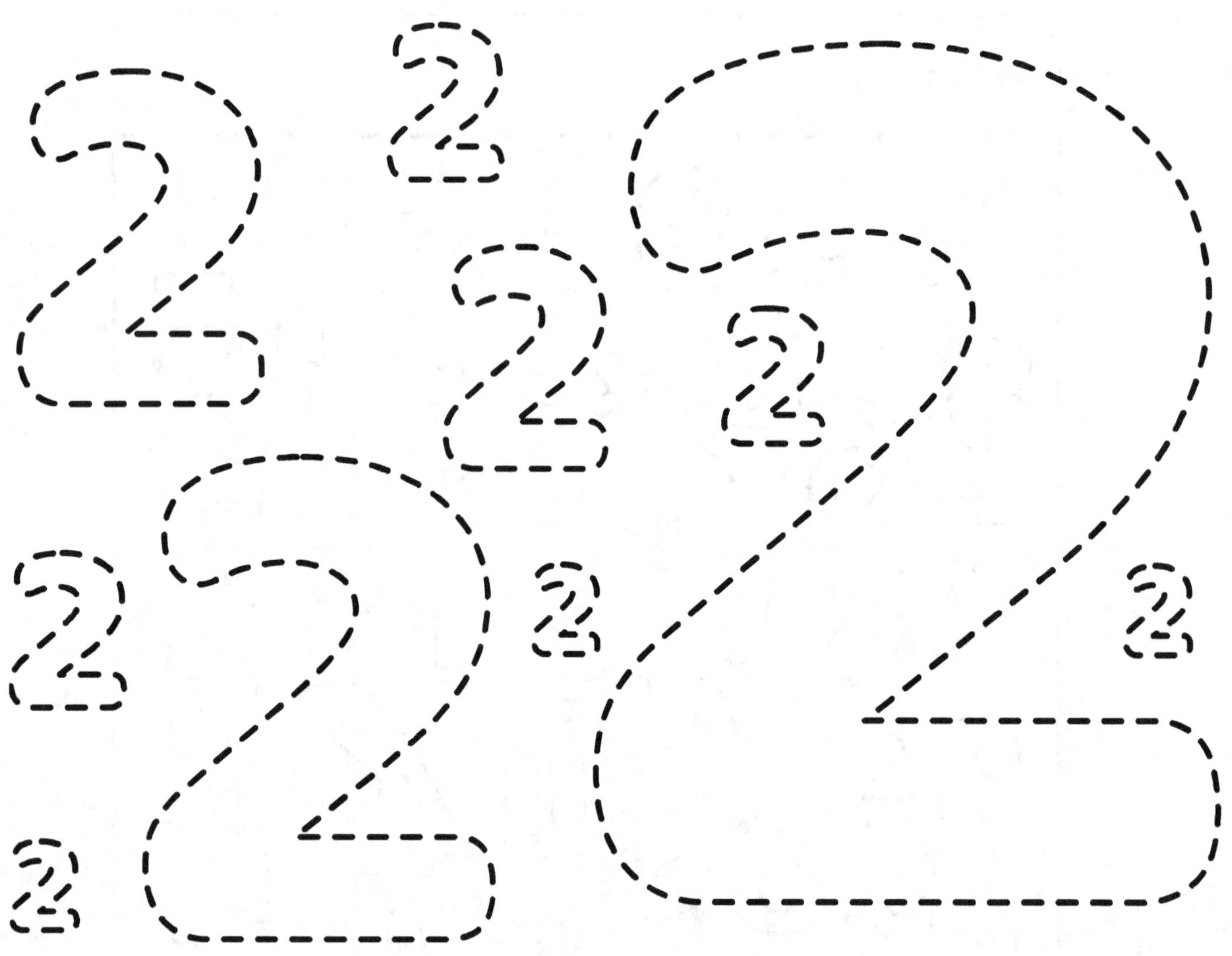

Name:

Date:

Trace:

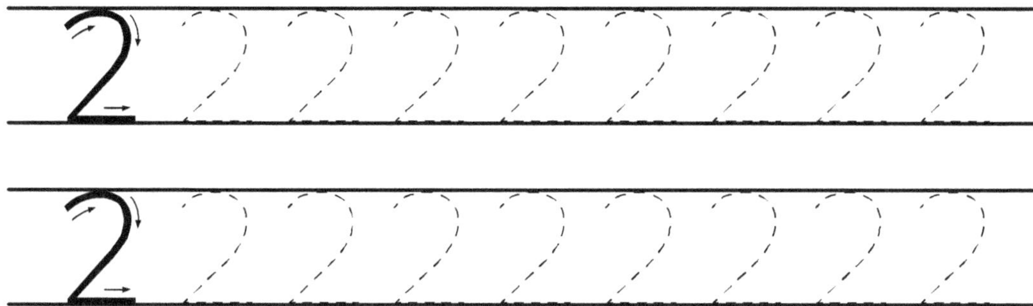

Find and color 2:

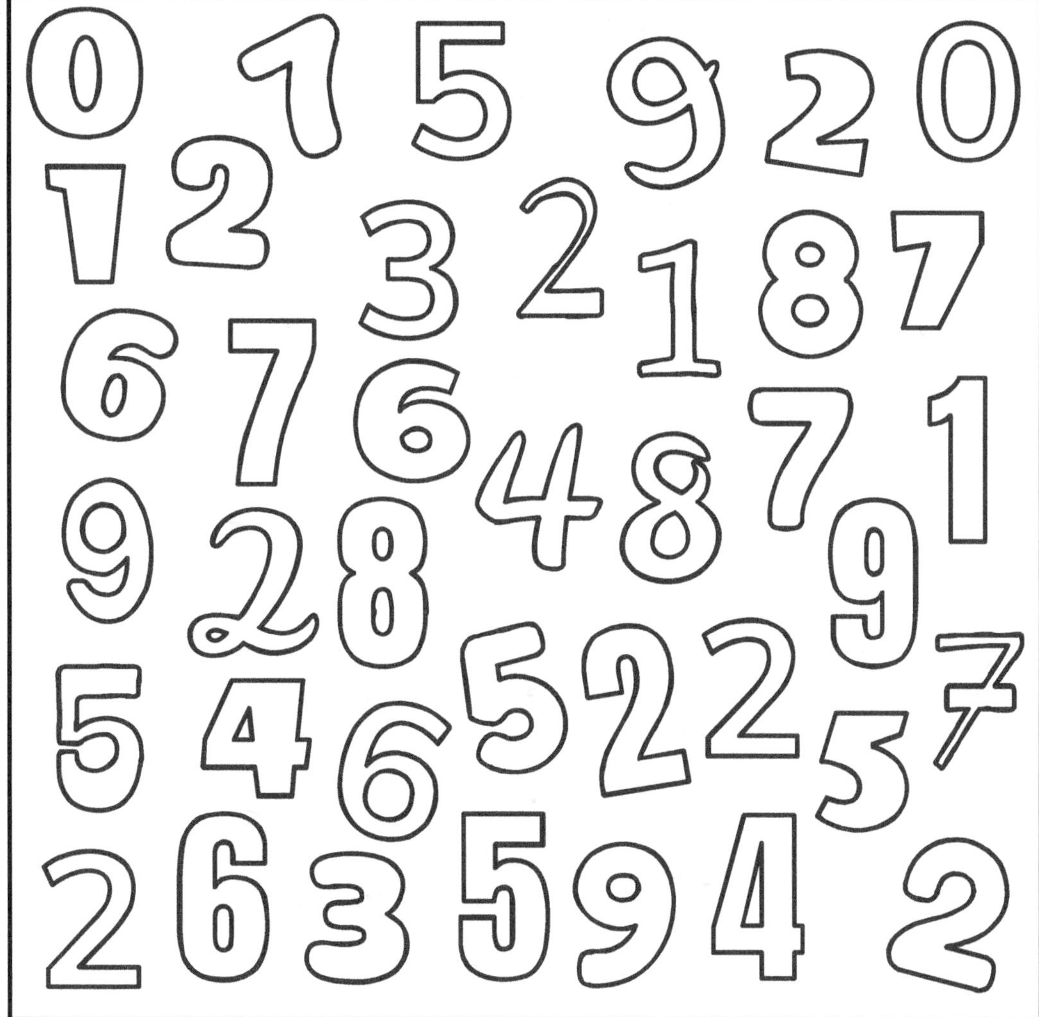

TRACE THE NUMBER

Trace the cell completely, to reveal the number 3

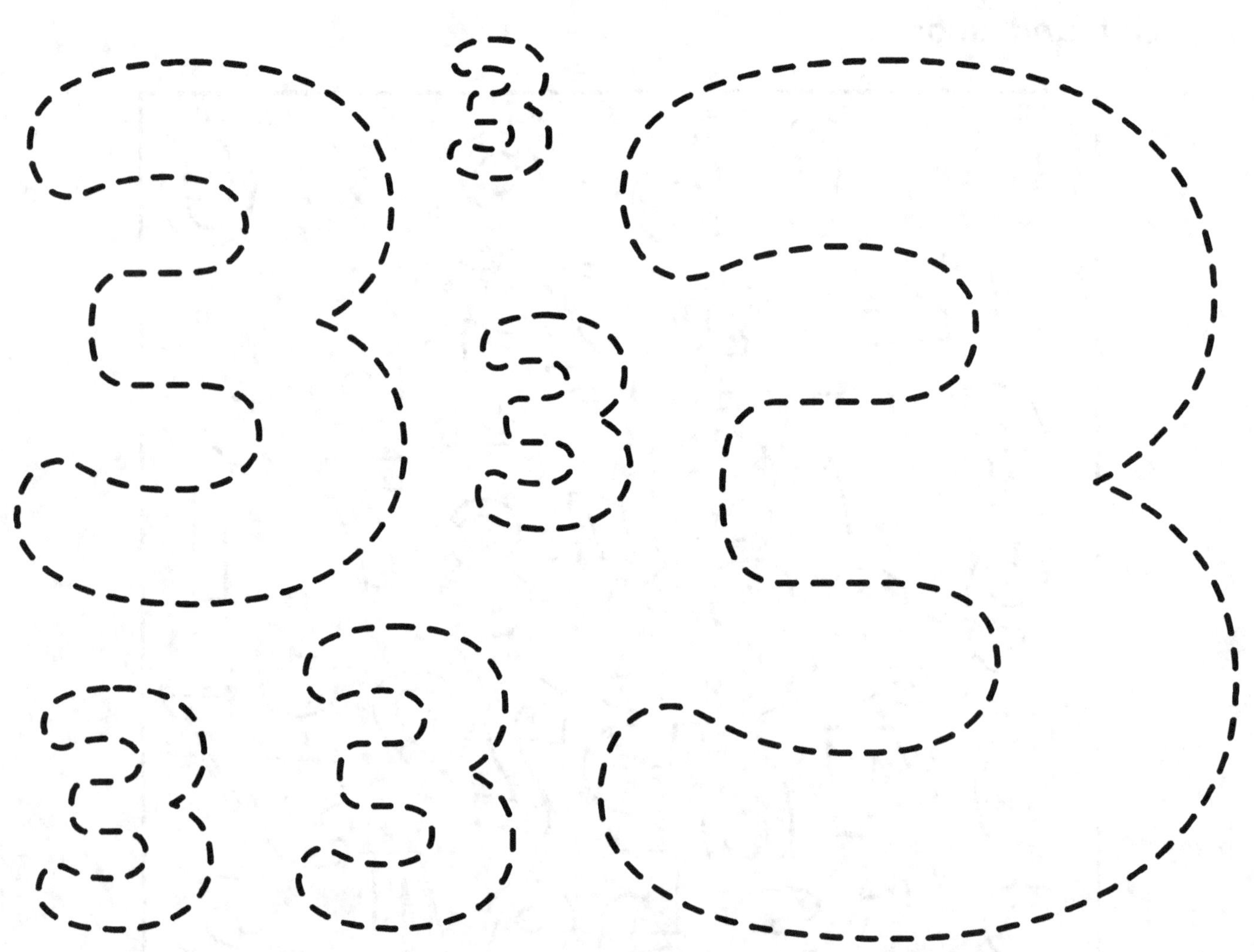

Trace:

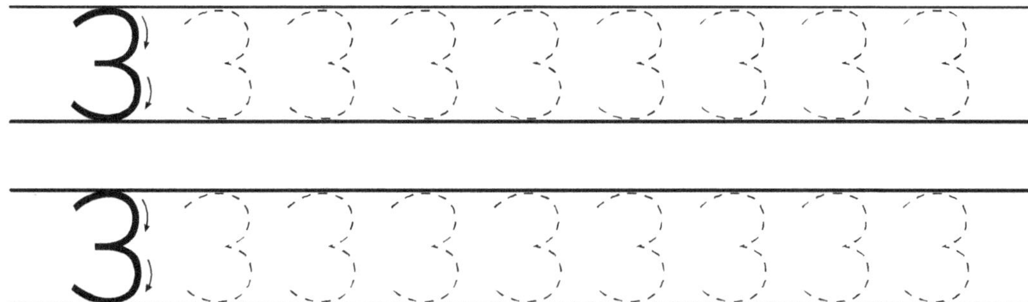

Find and color 3:

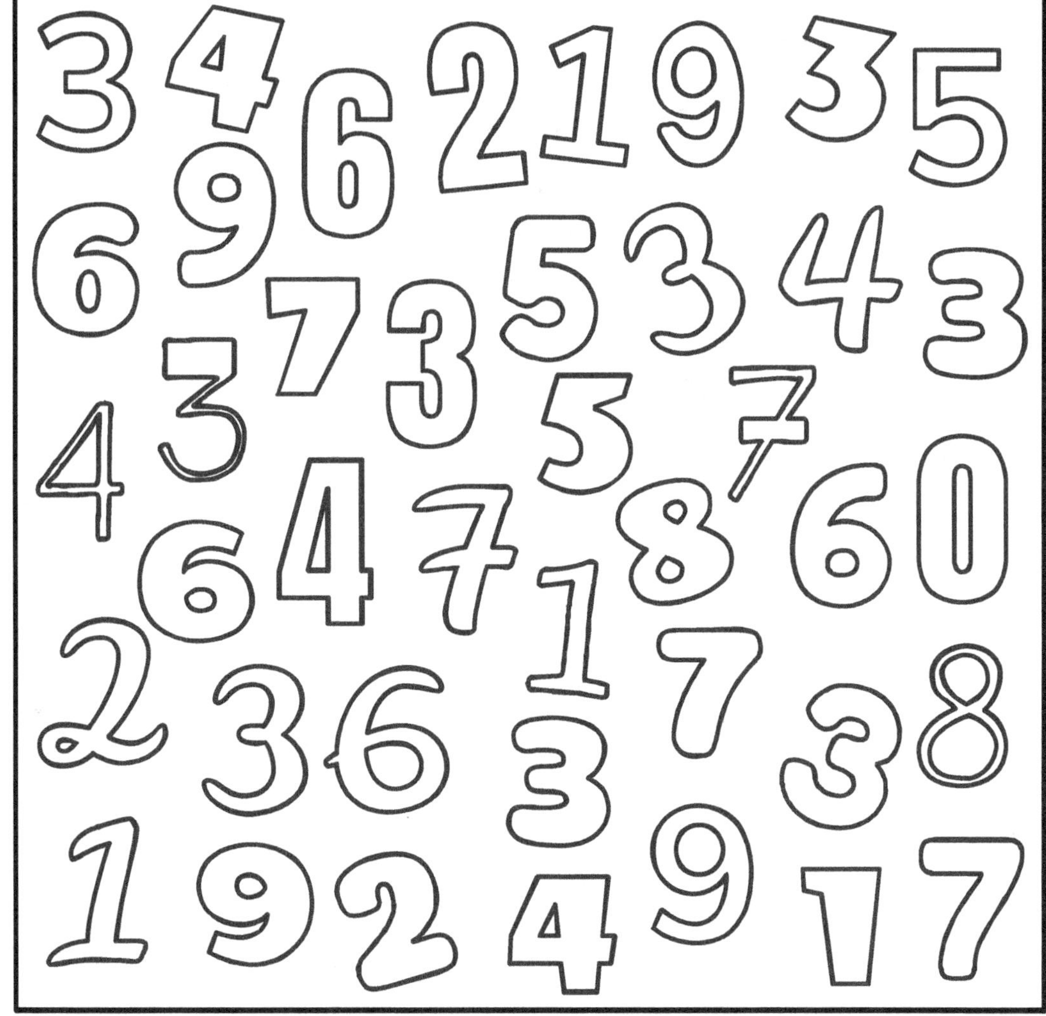

TRACE THE NUMBER

Trace the cell completely, to reveal the number 4

Name:

Date:

Trace:

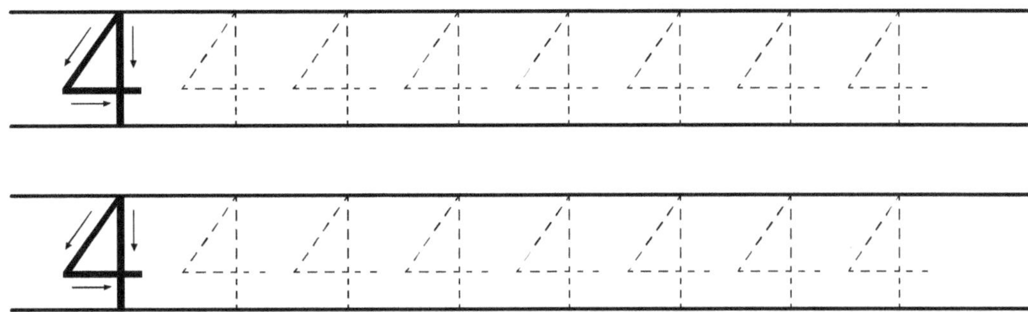

Find and color 4:

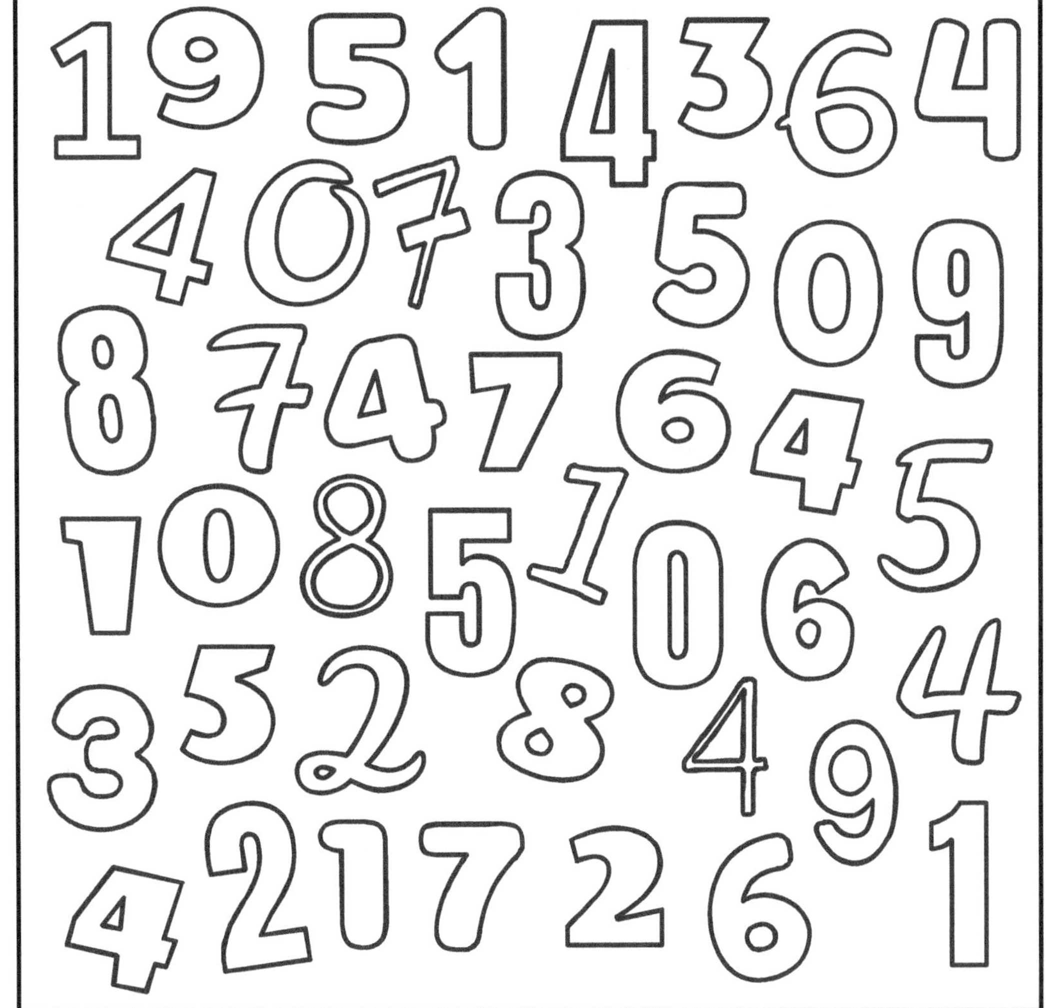

TRACE THE NUMBER

Trace the cell completely, to reveal the number 5

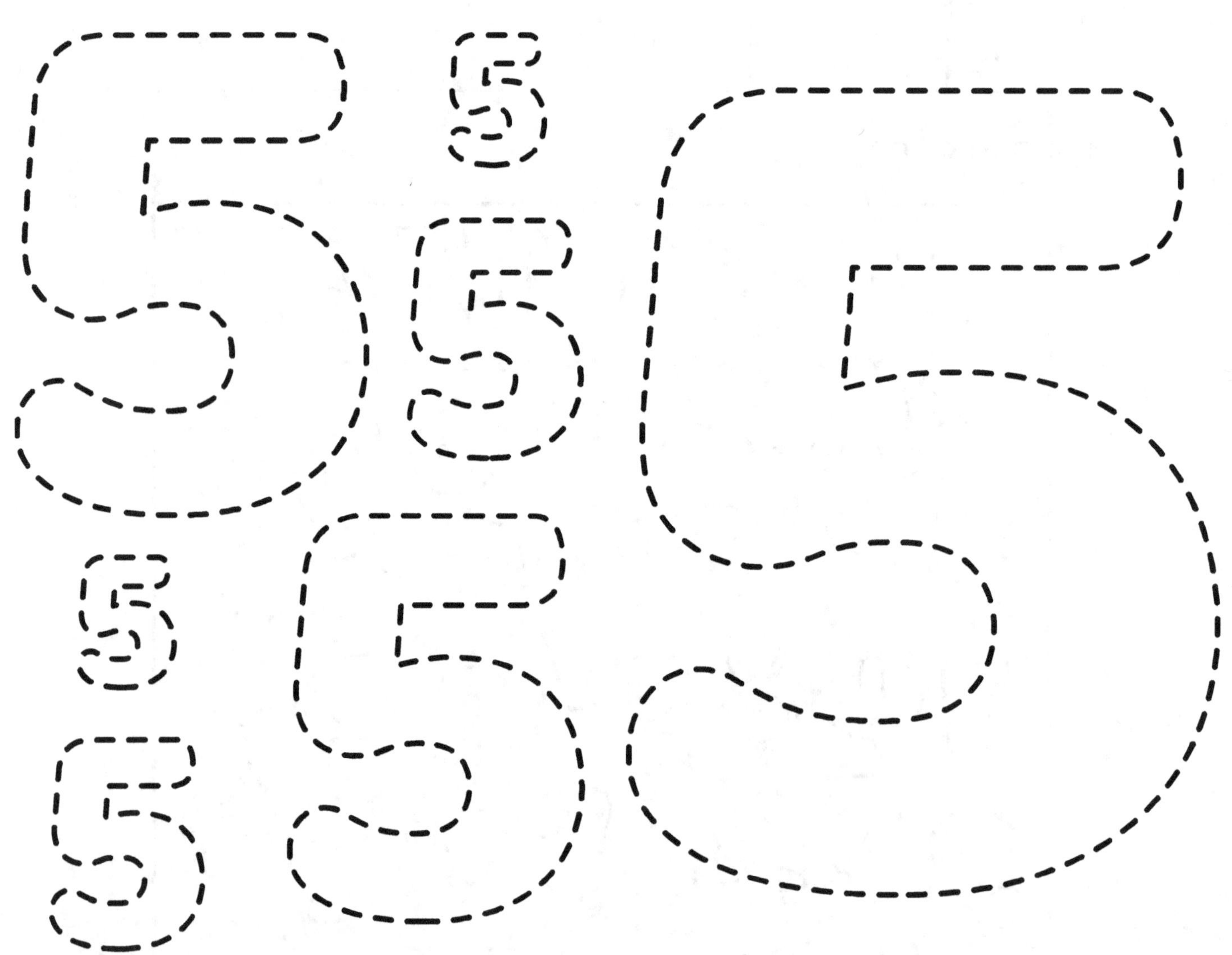

5

Trace:

5 5 5 5 5 5 5 5 5

5 5 5 5 5 5 5 5 5

Find and color 5:

TRACE THE NUMBER

Trace the cell completely, to reveal the number 6

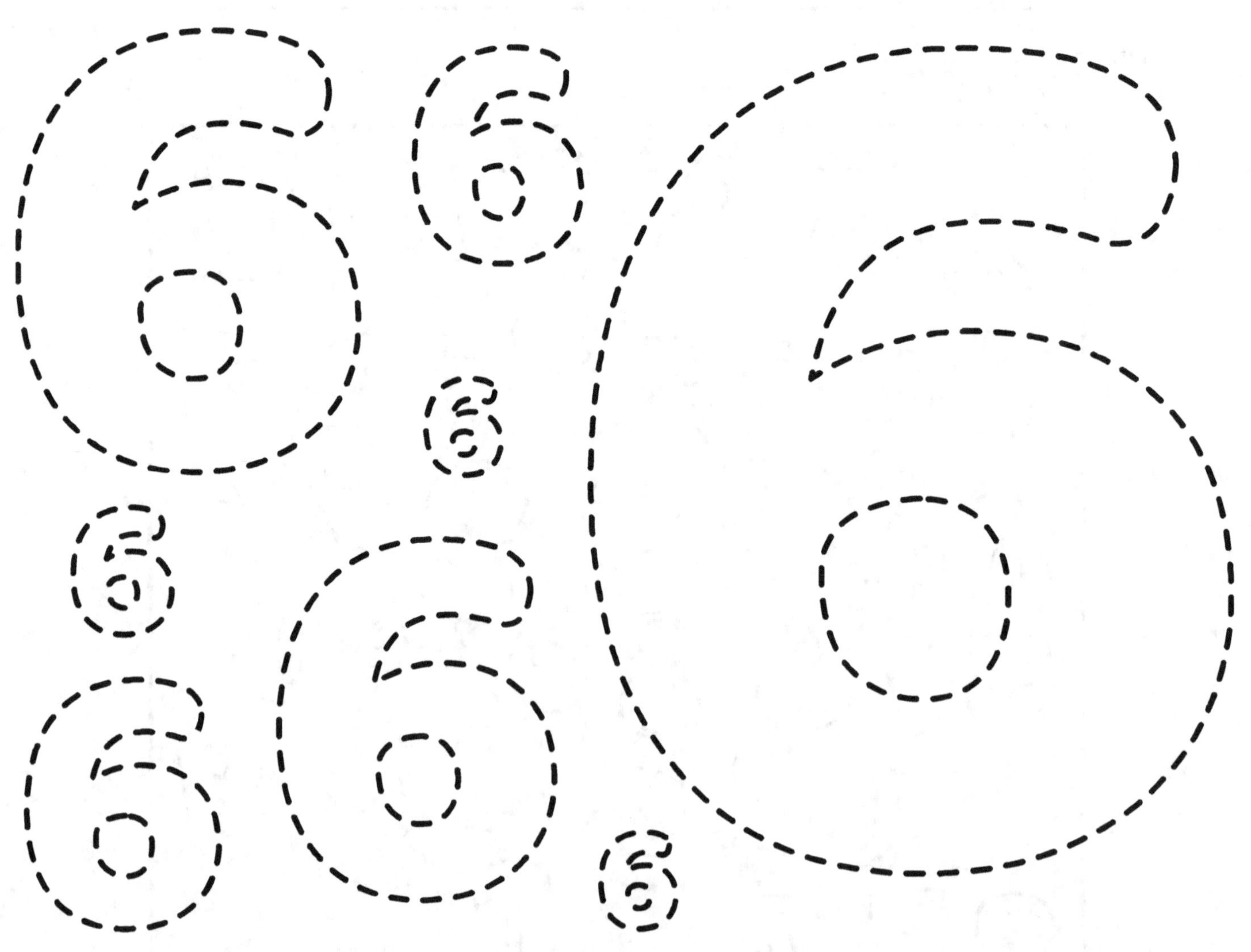

Trace:

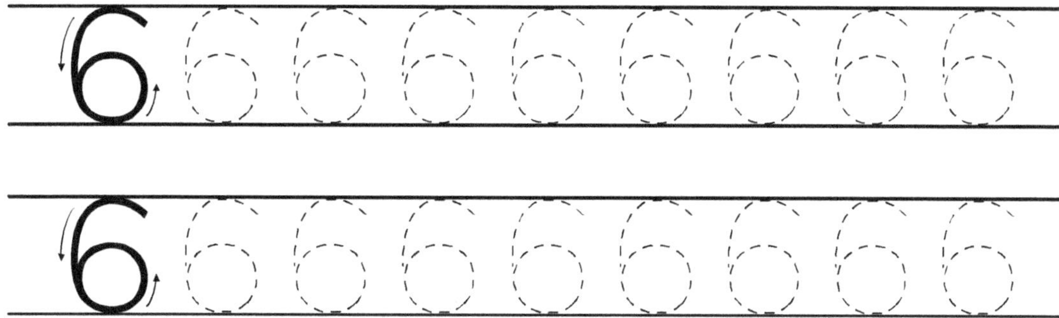

Find and color 6:

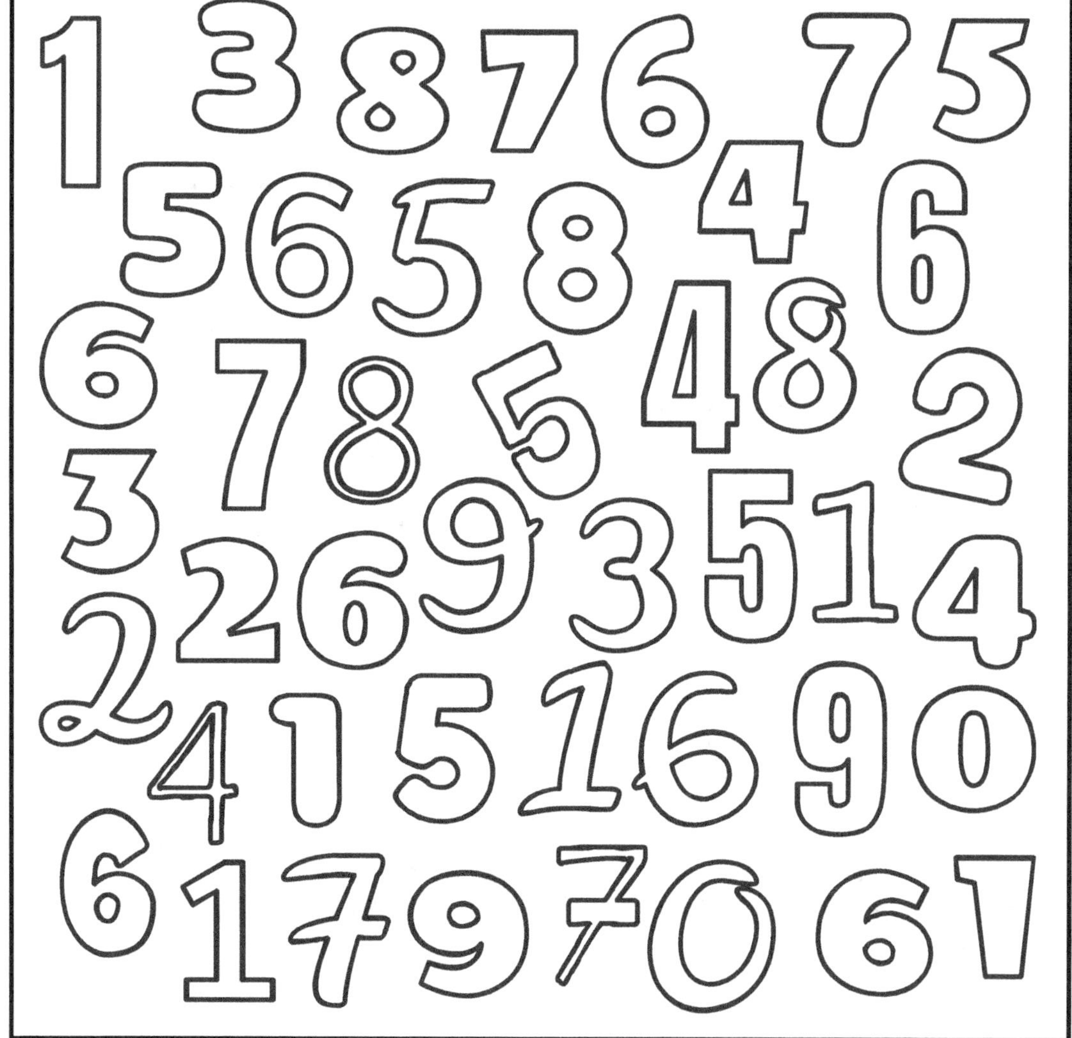

TRACE THE NUMBER

Trace the cell completely, to reveal the number 7

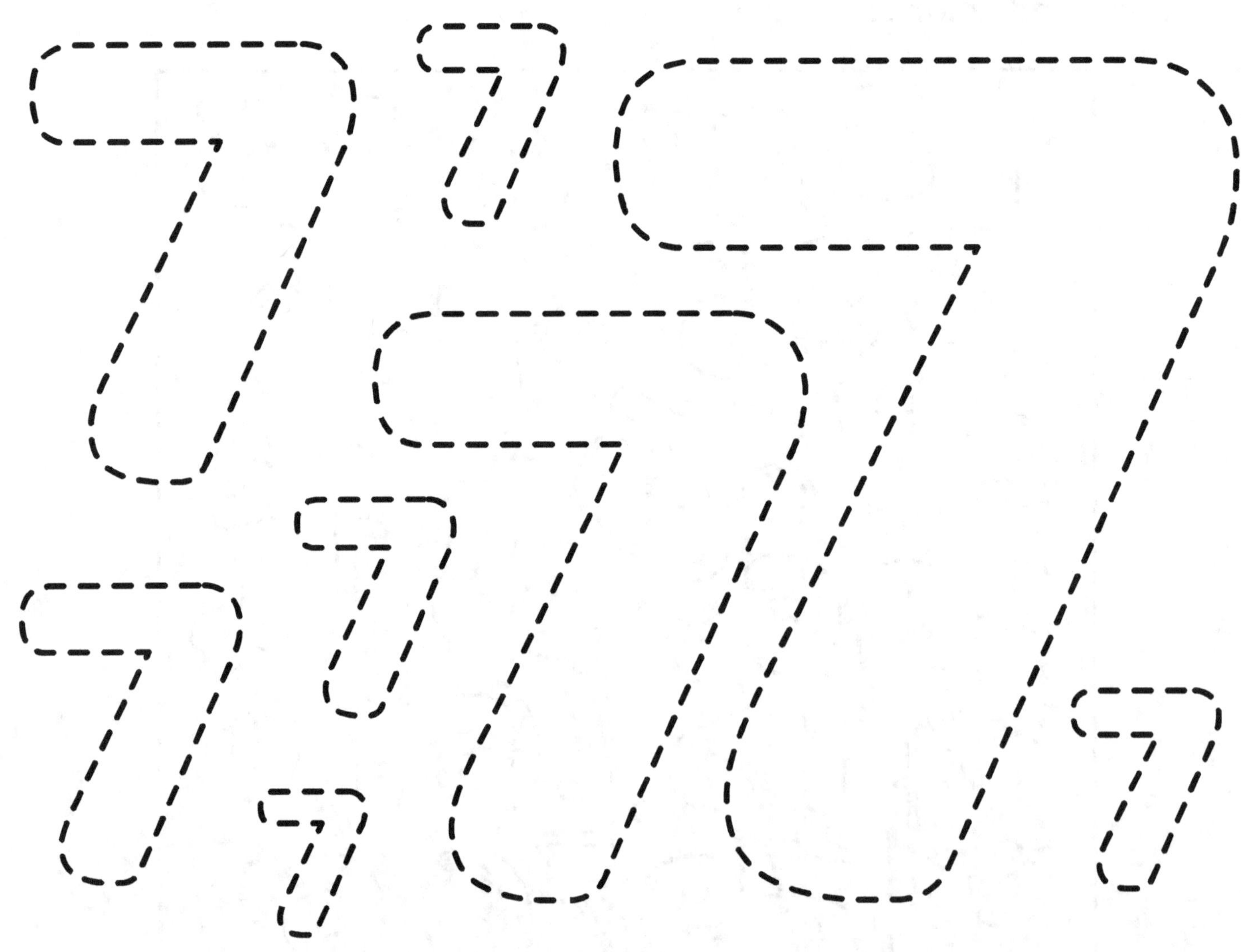

Trace:

Find and color 7:

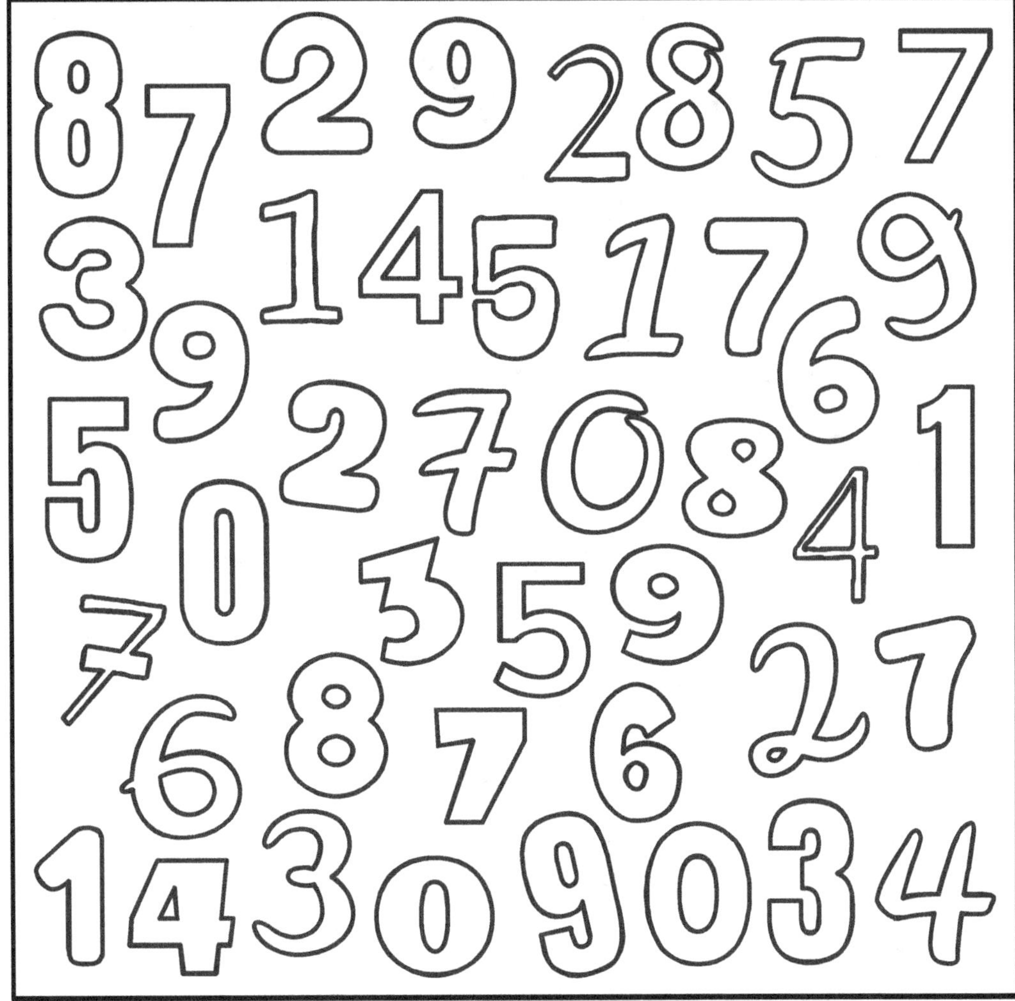

TRACE THE NUMBER

Trace the cell completely, to reveal the number 8

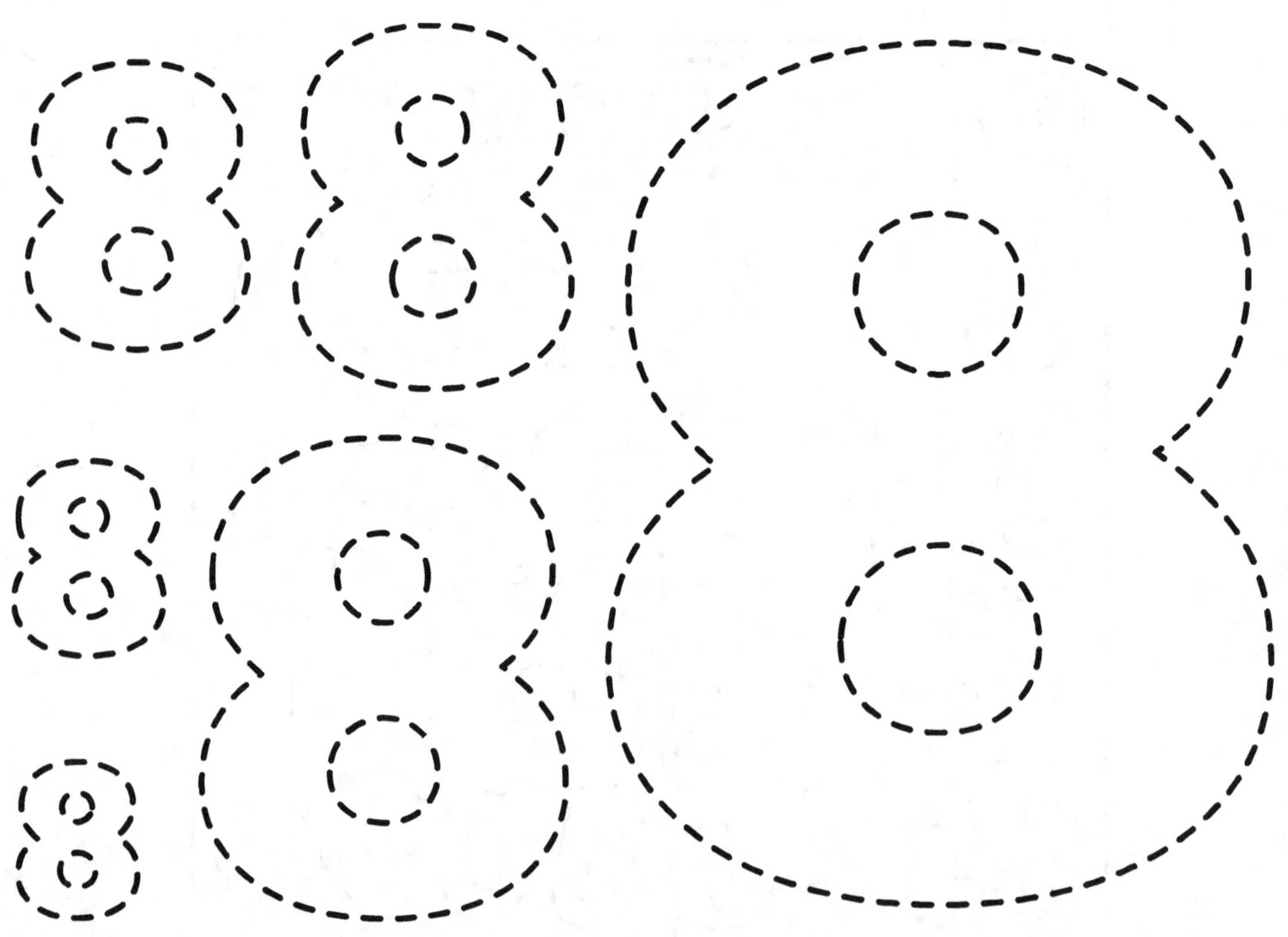

Trace:

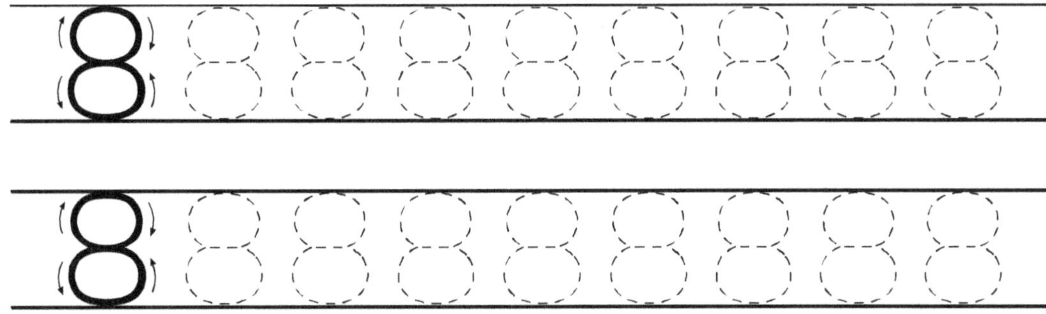

Find and color 8:

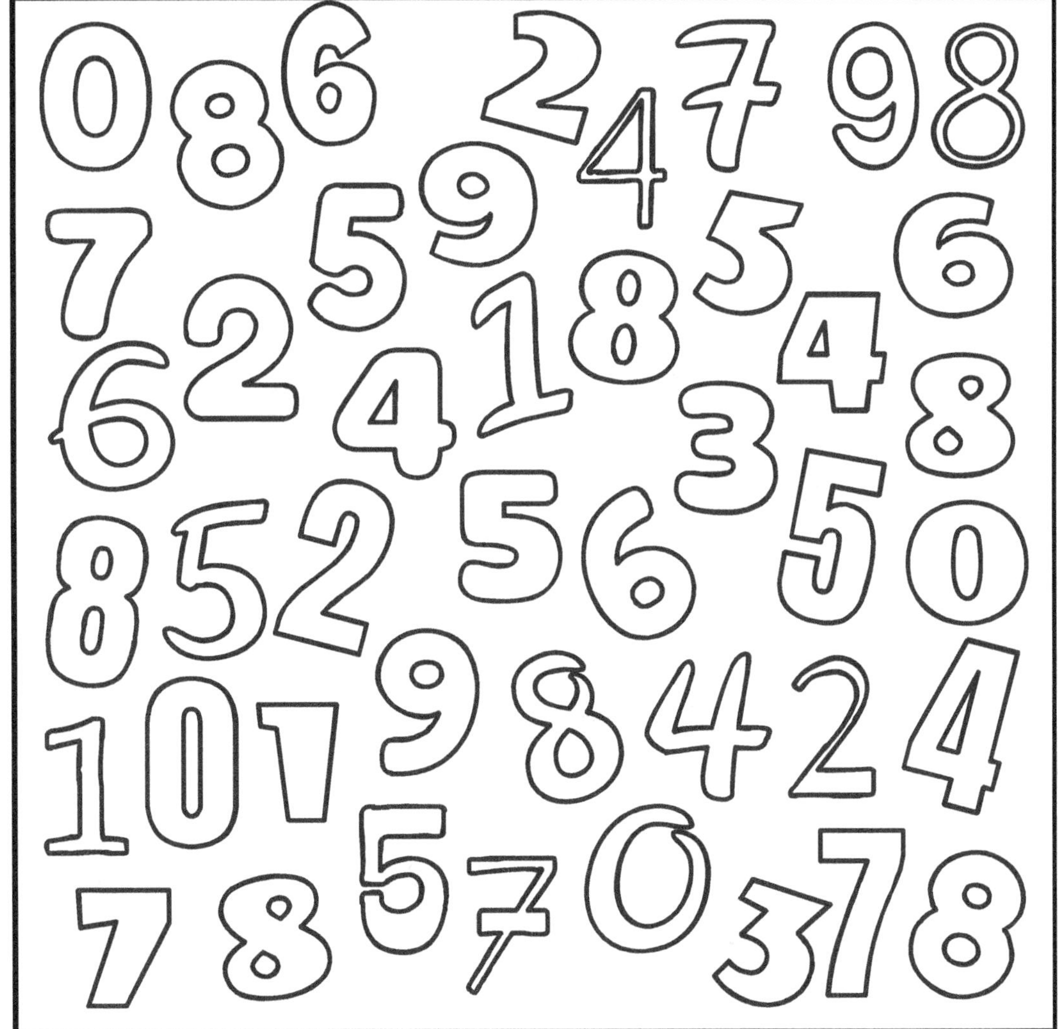

TRACE THE NUMBER

Trace the cell completely, to reveal the number 9

Trace:

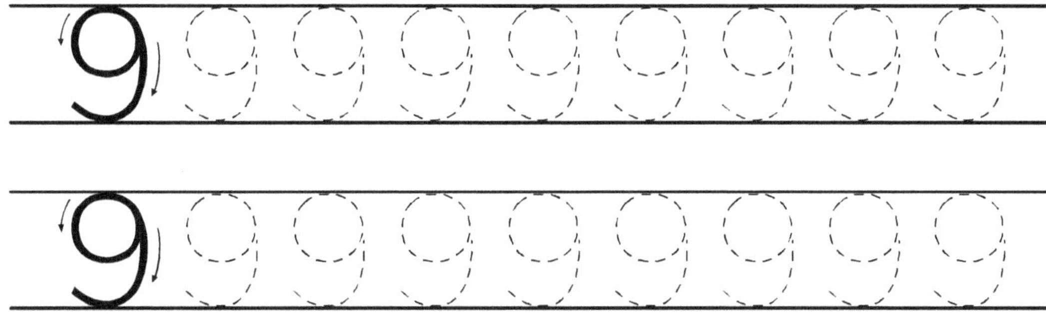

Find and color 9:

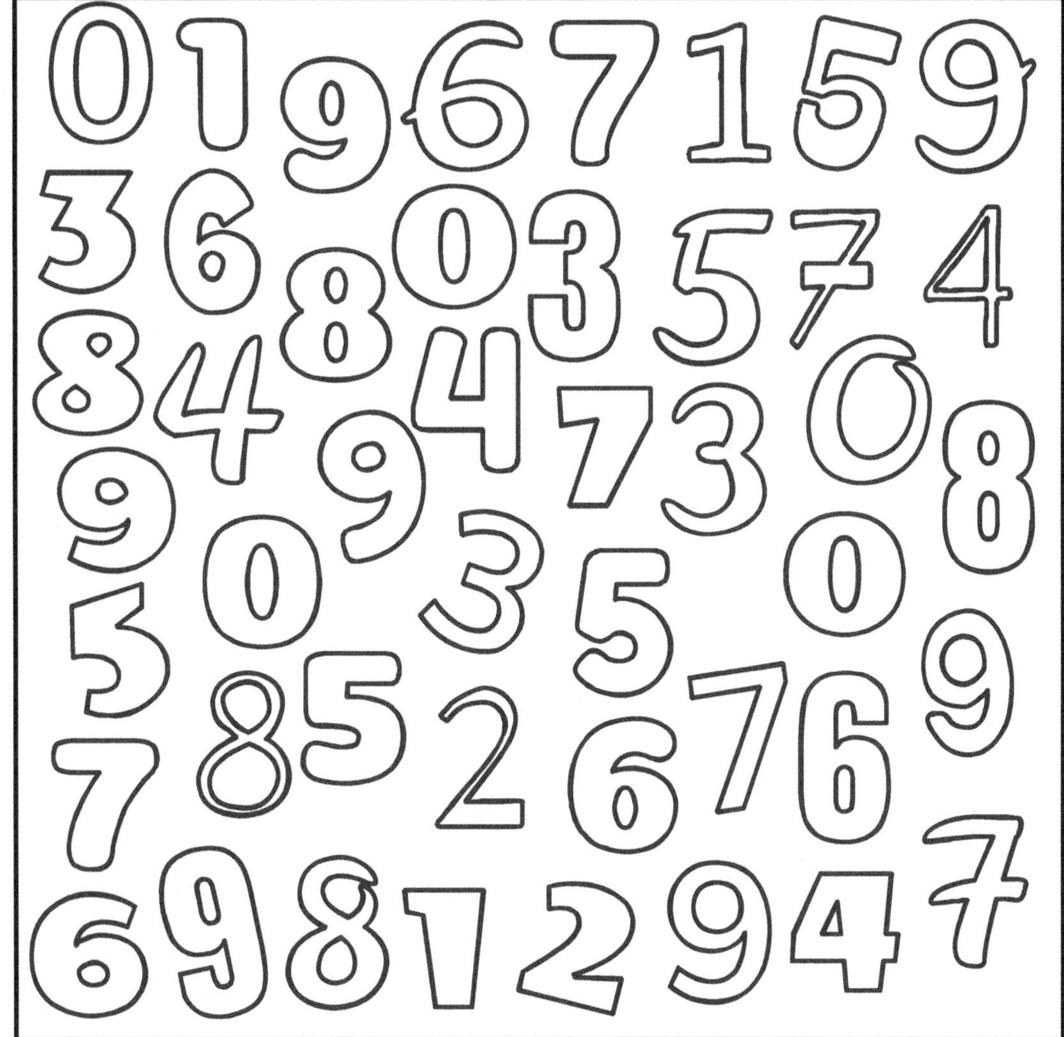

TRACE THE NUMBER

Trace the cell completely, to reveal the number 10

Check out more of our kids coloring and activity books !

Coloring Crafts Publications